A Kind of Knowing

A KIND OF KNOWING
conversations with spiritual healer

Floyd McAuslan

compiled & edited
by
Larry Kimmel

A Kind of Knowing

Copyright © 2007 by Larry Kimmel
All Rights Reserved

Acknowledgment is made to *"Country Journal, Huntington, Massachusetts"* where some these articles first appeared.

Published by
Winfred Press
364 Wilson Hill Road
Colrain, MA 01340
winfred@crocker.com
http://larrykimmel.tripod.com/

ISBN-13 : 978-0-9792484-0-5
ISBN-10 : 0-9792484-0-X

Dedicated To

T. C. Russell

Part 1 Introduction (Purpose and Intent of Book) / 1
    - 2 - Background: Floyd McAuslan, His Early Years / 3

Part 2 Thought Process, Meditation, and Concentration / 16

Part 3 About the Fare-Thee-Well Wholeness Center / 28

Part 4 The "Country Journal" Essays / 35
    - 2 - Essay 1, "Notes Toward Spiritual Virtuosity" / 37
    - 3 - Essay 2, "Thoughts Toward Peace" / 39
    - 4 - Essay 3, "Consider the Lilies" / 43
    - 5 - Five Principles of Fare-Thee-Well / 46

Part 5 Thoughts On a Spiritual Community / 47
    - 2 - Essay 4, "Isn't it all `Jest for Pun'" / 52

Part 6 The Practices of Healing / 55

Part 7 Exorcism and Protection / 73

Part 8 Other Spiritual Practices / 85
    - 2 - Triune Self / 86
    - 3 - Following Your Innate Desire / 90
    - 4 - Essay 5, "A Journey Begins with a Single Step" / 93
    - 5 - Application / 95
    - 6 - Moments of Fear / 98
    - 7 - Essay 6, "The Straight Life Has Rewards / 101

Part 9 Questions Concerning the Paranormal / 105

Part 10 Further Experiences in Parapsychology / 116

Part 11 Most Important Thing / 129

Part 12 "The Light of a Distant Hill" / 135

A KIND OF KNOWING
conversations with spiritual healer

Floyd McAuslan

PART ONE

This book is about the life, work, and philosophy of a Spiritual Healer. And in the telling of this man's life and work, my aim will be to stress the importance of thought in our daily lives, and the knowing that comes through the application of Creative Spiritual Thought. Why? Because we create our health, our happiness, our very circumstances through thought. Heaven and hell, I think, are not so much places, as states of mind. However, a state of mind can take us to some very real places, as I will show you.

Twenty years ago, if I had been told that I would find myself sitting, some Sunday morning, in a small "New Age" meeting place on a hillside property bounded by woodland, I would have dismissed it out of hand. Yet there I was, in the winter of 1981, sitting in a small meeting place that was, in fact, a drying shed with jars of herbs shelved along the walls and comfrey hanging from the ceiling.

Both a wood stove and a fireplace were in use that day. The fireplace was stone-faced and above it hung a bright mandala. On another wall hung a beautiful work of calligraphy. I would learn later that this document contained the five principles on which this organization, calling itself Fare-Thee-Well, was founded.

I had heard Floyd McAuslan, a founder and the Spiritual Director of Fare-Thee-Well, speak a month before. The occasion had been one of a series of guest speakers to PARA, an organization interested in the paranormal, at that time meeting in the Amherst area of western Massachusetts.

A friend had told me of "this healer from up in Huntington," and I had gone to hear him speak. The first words out of his mouth that evening were: "You are Light, Color, and Sound." And I was hooked. It was as though I had been waiting to hear these words spoken.

And why was I there, and why were these words important to me, and why did I subsequently find myself at Fare-Thee-Well, one winter Sunday morning? Because a long long sequence of thoughts had brought me step by step to the middle of a marsh and had left me stranded. I was bogged down by my own lack of awareness as to where I had been headed, and now I was looking for stepping stones back to solid ground.

That was fourteen years ago. Now I would like to share some of the benefit that I have found in Mr. McAuslan's teachings. There are many books on Healing, the Spiritual Path, and so on, but it is a message that can never be told too often. It needs not only retelling, but retelling in new and fresh ways, coming from many different viewpoints.

I say this last because I have found that, on the average, one out of five books on any given subject will speak to me more clearly than the others—a book written by a mind with a similar Thought Process to my own, I suppose. In any case, it became my thought to share some of Mr. McAuslan's knowledge on the Creative Spiritual Life by way of a book length interview.

Mr. McAuslan, an active speaker, healer, and counselor, has

had little time to write, so that when I proposed a book by interview his response was enthusiastic. He told me that he "had long wanted to extend his reach by means of a book."

Since so much of his Creative Spiritual Life was involved with the Healing Center, Fare-Thee-Well, I thought I might concentrate on that period of his career, and work in other elements of his spiritual adventures, such as his early years in the Spiritualist Church, stemming from the tradition of Sir Arthur Conan Doyle, and also his years on the road with Arthur Ford. And go from there to the philosophy he teaches and practices; his experiences of the paranormal; the methods he has found valid in the Art of Healing; as well as basic advice for Meditation and Concentration. But first we agreed to begin with some background.

What follows, then, has been constructed from a transcript of Mr. McAuslan's experiences with life on planet Earth from birth on up to the time of his leadership at Fare-Thee-Well.

• • •

- 2 -
Background

Though public speaking has played a large part in Floyd McAuslan career, he began his life as "a very quiet, very shy child," to the extent that he took failing grades in school rather then get up in front of the class and speak, even though he knew the material. In fact, he did not speak at all until the age of three, when pointing, as he always did, to what he wanted on the dinner table, he was asked point blank what it was he wanted. He spoke right out for the first time in a complete sentence.

Floyd further tells us that he started out in life with a tremendous fear of what would happen to him if his parents weren't around anymore. He was told in later years that when left with a baby sitter he would cry the entire evening till his parents returned. He still feels that this fear may have resulted because of a mishandling at birth, one that had necessitated his having to have three transfusions, which in 1929 was not so common as today.

When I asked if this difficult beginning had any bearing on his choice of profession as a healer in later life, he answered by saying that what did have a profound effect on his life, that in time, brought him to an awareness of Spiritual Healing, happened when he was twelve or thirteen years old.

At that time he developed a problem with epilepsy. Up to that point there had been no hint of such a problem, nor was it a family trait. He remembers that he was not only very concerned, but that he also had no idea in what direction to go.

However, the events that stemmed from this condition did lead to Mr. McAuslan's eventual work in the field of the paranormal, which I will let him tell in his own words:

• • •

"One day, when I was helping my parents around the house, I went out to empty the garbage in a pail, and I heard my aunt's voice, who had passed on a year or so before. At that time I had never experienced anything like that. But the voice, which I would say was my Aunt Christina's voice, just simply said to go downstairs to the cellar and to dust off the bookshelves, which I did.

"And as I was dusting off the bookshelves, I put my hand on a book, pulled it out, brought it upstairs and looked at it. It was a book on Christian Science, "Science and Health with Key to the Scriptures," by Mary Baker Eddie, which many people are familiar with. I opened it up to read it, and I had a really difficult time with it. I couldn't comprehend it. It didn't make much sense. But I did read it."

• • •

    This extra-perceptual experience resulted in his decision to go to a Christian Science Church, a year later, where he also attended their Sunday School. What he found there became the foundation for his Spiritual growth from there on in.
    "I felt I had gained much in the meaningfulness of what divine love is," he told me, adding that "in each of their churches, wherever you go all over the world, they say God is Love. And that message did permeate my consciousness."

• • •

    For the next three years, he attended a Christian Science Church and practiced Christian Science philosophy, but the cure he was hoping for did not take place. The epilepsy stayed about the same.
    Then one day, his mother attended a service at the Spiritualist Church in Springfield, Massachusetts with a friend of hers who had lost a daughter and hoped to find some solace in the matter.
    Floyd remembers his mother reporting that she had heard from her brother, George, and that he had said some things to her. And, also, that her friend, the woman who had lost her daughter, had also received what they called a "message." It was a message from her daughter, Betty, to the effect that Betty was, in fact, very much alive and well, though concerned about her mother's sorrow over her passing on. These messages had been given through a Mr. T. C. Russell, who would soon become an important figure in Floyd's life.
    Floyd said that he became "quite interested to hear such strange things," and so he asked a friend of his if he would be willing to go with him to experience this phenomenon, "or whatever it was." So they went down to the Spiritualist Church on

Bliss Street.

"I just wanted to sit in the back row and experience whatever seemed to be happening," he told me, and went on to say that Mr. Russell gave that day what he considered a very excellent lecture about life here and the life hereafter.

When Mr. Russell went into the message end of the program, Floyd, "was expecting to see some kind of angelic host, or ghosts, or whatever, coming out from the walls, which they didn't." Nonetheless he did received a message. Again, it was from his mother's brother, his Uncle George.

"Nobody at the church, or Mr. Russell, had experienced us before," he explained. "They didn't know me, or my friend, or any of our families. We were there for the first time. So I became quite interested."

• • •

This was done in May, and Floyd was informed that Mr. Russell would be at a nearby place for the month of August. So in August he and his mother went to Lake Pleasant, Massachusetts, where his mother had a sitting with Mr. Russell. She, of course, was concerned about her son's epilepsy. Mr. Russell told her that in a year to a year-and-a-half Floyd would be completely healed of epilepsy. His mother, he recalls, was quite elated to hear that, and that he, himself, also spoke with Mr. Russell at that time.

Mr. Russell, he said, "kind of took me under his wing. I was seventeen at the time. He talked to me about Healing and Meditation and so forth, and I found it all very plausible. I felt very comfortable with Mr. Russell. He was an Episcopalian by faith, but the Spiritualist Church was the only place where he could share his talent."

After a year of study with Mr. Russell, either by being personally with him or by letter, Mr. Russell asked Floyd if he would be willing to do some Healing, to which Floyd answered by saying that he "didn't really know anything about it. Not enough to speak of." But Mr. Russell told him to just come up on the platform on a Sunday evening and try it.

"I was eighteen at that time," Floyd went on to say, "and I still had the epilepsy. But I did what I felt was a comfortable thing in relationship to Healing. I had people come forward, talked with them, and then laid hands on them.

"Afterward, I heard that one of the women I had worked with claimed to have been healed of breast cancer. I don't know whether she was or not, because she did not say this to me directly. This is what other people told me a year later."

• • •

In the following year, Floyd found that the epilepsy had fallen away. "It didn't seem to be occurring as often as it had, but I wasn't sure that it might not re-occur in the future. I just didn't know." But as time went on he found that Mr. Russell had been absolutely accurate in what he had said. The epilepsy was gone, and gone completely.

Floyd was still going to the Christian Science Church, but in studying their literature more closely he found that they spoke disparagingly of Spiritualism. He said that he just couldn't understand why they would take that particular organization and knock it against all the others that were around.

At the same time he took a closer look into the Spiritualist's Movement. It was about this time that Arthur Ford would be lecturing in New York City. Floyd thought that he might go down to hear him, because he'd heard that Ford had been directed by Sir Arthur Conan Doyle, and that Ford was the most outstanding medium and lecturer in the world.

"My thought," Floyd said, "was that I might as well get into that right now." This was to be a destined decision that I will, again, let Mr. McAuslan tell in his own words:

. . .

"Arthur Ford was in the 1st World War. And one day in a foxhole a scroll was presented before him in a visionary process. It gave many names, and he noticed that they were all names of the men who were around him where he was serving in France.

"The following day he found that all the men whose names he had seen in this scroll had been killed. This happened for three days in a row, and finally he couldn't contain himself and told his commanding officer that he needed a leave of absence to go to London.

"They gave him a short leave of absence, and he went over to London and inquired of Sir Arthur Conan Doyle, because he knew that Doyle was involved with this type of thing. And he did get a chance to see Doyle, who was very excited with what Ford had to tell him. Sir Arthur Conan Doyle told Ford to come and see him when he got out of the service after the war, and that he would send him to the right person to develop his talent.

"So after the war, Ford did just that. He saw Sir Arthur Conan Doyle, and Doyle sent him to India for training in Meditation, Concentration, and so forth. He was there, I believe, for about a year. When he returned to the United States in 1925, he had one additional year of classes with Yogananda.

"The first time that Ford went into trance was during one of Yogananda's classes. It seems he spoke to different people there in the group. And after he came out of his trance, he wondered what had happened. He thought he had fallen asleep. Yogananda told him that he had gone into trance and had spoken about different people.

"Yogananda also told him to remember that that was just one of the many facets of Spiritual experience and not to get all puffed up about it, that it was no big deal. But Ford thought that it was a pretty good thing.

"Ford had been brought up a fundamentalist and had been going to a very basic Christian college before he went into the service and, of course, they frowned upon anything of that type happening to anyone. But he felt he should take it up, and so he did.

"He started giving messages, communications, all very very accurate. The messages were always communications from people on the other side known to the people receiving the messages. There weren't discussions with Guides or people that they didn't know. The people sending the messages were always loved ones, or had some connection with the person receiving the message. Always there was some sort of direct contact. These were not messages from famous personalities, or shamans, or the like.

"He acquired during that time a control, that is, one who spoke through him when he was in trance, whose name was Fletcher. Fletcher wasn't the real name of his control, but Fletcher wanted the name he had use on Earth to be disguised because of his parents, who were Roman Catholics from Florida.

"Fletcher had been a boyhood friend of Ford's, and had been killed at the age of twelve or thirteen. And so Fletcher made a commitment to Arthur Ford, saying that as long as Ford was in the body, he, Fletcher, would stay with Ford and be his control. Which he did. He stayed with Ford to the very end."

• • •

"When I went to the first lecture in New York City and heard Arthur Ford, there were several hundred people there, and he gave a lecture and then gave maybe six messages, and one of the messages was to me. He told me either I was or would be involved with Spiritual Healing.

"Afterwards, I went up to him and told him how much I'd enjoyed his lecture, how it was very good, but how he was inaccurate on what he had said to me about Healing, because I didn't really know anything about it, and to make it my life, well, it just didn't make sense.

"He didn't discuss it or argue with me at all. He asked where I lived, and I told him, and he said that in a few months he would be at a Spiritualist Camp in Connecticut near Niantic, which was not too far from where I lived. He said that if I wanted to come down, he'd be there for a week, and that I was welcome to come and join in the services.

"Well, because of the lecture and the message, my appetite was whetted. He had quite a dynamic personality. So I took a week's vacation and went down to hear his lectures and, as it would happen, during the very first lecture he again had a message for me about Healing. He used essentially the same words he had used in New York City, and I was thinking as he was telling me this, `it's amazing, he must have a photographic memory, or something, because he certainly sees an awful lot of people and here, out of several hundred people, he can pinpoint me and remember what he said.'"

• • •

"So I went up to him, again, and said probably the same thing I'd said to him in New York City. And he kind of smiled and asked if I was going to stay there for the week, and I said yes. And so I went to all the services and all the lectures. He also invited me to come over and talk with him whenever I wanted to.

"Now at that time, I didn't realize what a privilege was happening to me. But, nonetheless, I took advantage of it. And in that week's time I learned a lot.

"I say I learned a lot because I felt right with it, you know. I'd heard a lot of things from other people by that time in regards to the Spiritual, but what he was saying made sense to me. Things that I had never heard before. They just kind of rang true. At the end of the week he asked if I was interested in doing some traveling with him. And I said, "Well yeah, I guess so."

"At the time I was going to school at the University of Massachusetts, so I called up my folks and told them the situation, and they said they'd put the money for my education into traveling with this man if that's what I wanted to do. So I did.

"In the meantime, of course, my parents got all kinds of calls saying what kind of a person this Arthur Ford was. That he wasn't sincere, and that you couldn't trust him, and so forth. Fortunately, my folks were great about all this. They had confidence in me. They felt that if anything was wrong with this man, I wouldn't be with him. And so I did some traveling, and helped him out at different times, working with him, selling his books, and so forth. This was around 1950 and '51.

"However, after a period of time, I had what I would call Spiritual indigestion. And so I left. I thanked Ford, of course, for what I had learned and let him know how appreciative I was of it all.

"My feeling was that if any of these Spiritual things were right, I would eventually get back into it. But I was just filled up to the eyebrows at that point. So I left the Spiritual Path for about three years, until I felt that I had to get back into it again. Which I did. I just couldn't help myself, I guess."

• • •

During those three years, however, Floyd did go to the August services, at Lake Pleasant, Massachusetts, which was the oldest established Spiritualist Camp ground in the world at that time. There he learned from and worked with Mr. T. C. Russell, who, as Floyd has already said, took him under his wing.

With Mr. Russell's guidance, Floyd did begin the practice of Healing there at Lake Pleasant, eventually taking over the Sunday evening Healing Services. "But that was the only association I had with the Spiritual during those years," he explained. "I wasn't doing any reading or anything else about it."

In 1955, at age twenty-five, however, Floyd became president of the Spiritualist Church, in Springfield, Massachusetts. "That is when I really first got back into the Spiritual way of things," he told me. He acted as President of the Spiritualist Church for one year before he opened a place of his own in relationship to Spiritual Healing at the Grange Hall in West Springfield.

From West Springfield, he went to the Science Museum in Springfield proper, where, because it was in the Science Museum, he had to have a name for his organization. He called it Infinite Science. Again it was pertaining primarily to Healing, and that was for two years.

During this time he married Priscilla Stephens and together they ran their own gift shop and produce stand at the Notch in Amherst, Massachusetts. Later, at the time when the first of his three children was born, he would sell this business and work with one of the major supermarket chains. Eventually he moved himself and his family from South Hadley to Worthington, Massachusetts.

But before that move, while still living in South Hadley, he and Priscilla were to experience another interesting paranormal phenomenon.

• • •

"My mother had passed on," he explained "and my father was still living in the house. And he invited Priscilla and me to live there with him, and so we did. This was before we had children.

"Any rate, I was upstairs, one day, and my wife was downstairs, and she called up the stairs and said, `Did you hear that, Floyd?' And I said, `Yes, I heard it.' And I said, `What did you hear?' `No, you tell me what you heard,' Priscilla answered. And I said, `No. You tell me what you heard.'

"Well, finally I said, `I heard my mother call my name.' And she said, `That's what I heard too.'

"That was the second time in my life that I had heard a voice from the other side," Floyd said, concluding this story, though adding, "I still, to this day, have never seen anyone or anything from the other side, not at a seance or anywhere."

• • •

When Floyd and Priscilla were settled in at Worthington, Massachusetts, they started another little gathering place, "because here we had, as we still do, a small structure on the grounds. We had services right out there," he told me, pointing to a small outbuilding, or good-sized shed, that sits at the far edge of an expanse of lawn that turns to field, with a view of mountains in the blue distance.

These services, Floyd explained, began as Healing Practices, but developed more and more into overall Spiritual practices, guidance, and eventually some counseling. At the same time, Floyd was still working for his livelihood as a produce manager.

"This went on for several years," he said, "till one day I saw in the newspaper that the minister who had married Priscilla and me had returned to the area. He was the head of the United Church of Christ in Hampden, Franklin, and Berkshire counties, and was stationed in Amherst, which is not too far from here. I called him and invited him up to supper one evening.

"We talked about general things. He told about his work and so forth, and then he asked what I was doing. Well, I couldn't really discuss too much of the technical thing I was doing, but I did say that I was into Spiritual areas. And then he said, `Why don't you get involved with the UCC, the United Church of Christ.' And I said, `Well I don't think so.'

"`Why don't you start off as a lay minister?' he asked me, and said that if I took a year's training at that, I could help them out at churches in the area when ministers were out sick, or whatever. Finally I said that I would. So I did."

• • •

Floyd trained under the UCC and studied their literature for a year and was approved by the Tri-County Board of the United Council of Churches as a lay minister, after which he went around to certain churches where they needed help. Usually, he would be at one or another of their churches for just a Sunday, and felt he could not accomplish much just being at a church for one Sunday. He also felt that he couldn't speak out about what he really believed under those circumstances. What he had to say would have been on the metaphysical direction and most of the people, he felt, would not comprehend it. This went on for three years.

• • •

Then a small church in Huntington, the next town over from Worthington, needed someone on a part-time basis, but full time on Sundays.

"I told them," he said, "that I was interested in parapsychology, and they said that that was fine with them. I don't really think they knew what it meant. Nonetheless, they took me on, or I took them on. I don't know which it was.

"They wanted some Bible study classes. So I said, `Why don't we start with the Apostles' Creed in your song book, since that is supposed to be one of your precepts.' So we went with what they had, which was pasted in the back of each of the song books.

"We studied about Angels, about Archangels, about Hell and Heaven, and so forth. We discussed these things, which they had never discussed before.

"Through this we got unto a good format. And that was our stepping stone for what came next. Instead of calling this a Bible study group, we called it a Spiritual Awareness group. Some left because of that, but for those who stayed it became a very special experience."

• • •

Floyd remained at the First Congregational Church of Huntington, Massachusetts for the next five years, and had built up the attendance till he and Priscilla had quadrupled the congregation. Priscilla was superintendent of the Sunday School. He remembers that they had built up the Christmas Eve service to overflowing.

"It was a good thing," he said. "We got a lot of activities going, a lot of suppers, a lot of creative things going, and, of course, our Spiritual Awareness class.

"Then one Sunday, I was standing in the pulpit and unbeknownst to me, I was standing there telling them that I was leaving. I just didn't know what to make of the situation. My wife didn't know either."

This announcement, this spontaneous decision, would mark the beginning of a whole new venture, a whole new approach to Floyd's ministry, that would, in time, become a Wholeness Center called Fare-Thee-Well.

Fare-Thee-Well, which means, "a state of perfection," is where I, the compiler of this book, first got to know Mr. McAuslan. But before I go on to tell about the Fare-Thee-Well experience, I would like to discuss some of the basic Spiritual practices that Mr. McAuslan teaches.

Also, at this point, Mr. McAuslan wishes it to be made clear that in this book he is sharing his experiences, but that they are only his experiences, and that what he has found to be true for him might not be true for someone else, and that he does not wish to imply that he has all the answers. "Others," he says, "should be aware that their experiences might be different."

PART TWO
Thought Process, Meditation, and Concentration

LK   It seems to me that "Thought Process" is one of the key phrases in your teaching. I have said in the introduction to this book that thought is everything. Why do you stress this idea? How far or deep are its ramifications?

FM   Thoughts are of the utmost importance to us. Perhaps more than anything else, where we keep our thoughts is where we keep the body, the mind, and the spirit.

   I think, Kirilian photography is a wonderful way to demonstrate the importance of Thought Process. In this type of photography a picture is taken of the whole person, and done in such a way that the light and energy emanating from the body of that person is shown. You will see it extending outwardly from the body, particularly from the hands and fingertips. And it quite discreetly describes where that person's thinking and feelings are at that moment.

   For example, in a class on Meditation that I was conducting at the University of Massachusetts, I asked a young woman to meditate for a period of time. Then a picture was taken with this Kirilian type of photography. As expected, we found very special, very wonderful emanations coming from her body. Beautiful colors. Beautiful energies. Whites, purples, greens, and so forth.

   Then she was told, by someone who she knew to be psychic, that she was pregnant. Now remember, this was a young woman who was not married. So she was told that she was pregnant and then another picture was taken. This time there were no emanations of beautiful color. The picture was black. Nothing came out. There was no energy. It was as if the whole body had been short circuited. And all this had come about from the thought that she was pregnant.

It shows how quickly our thoughts can alter our energies, and tells us what we can do in an instant with thought.

We all know what it is like to be in a social situation feeling perfectly fine until suddenly something is said that embarrasses us. Immediately we blush or even perspire. And yet the words spoken were simply sounds. The interpretation was our own.

This, I feel, is reason enough to recognize, at all times, that life is truly good, that the beauty of the Infinite is us. Is us. With us. Around us. Above us. Below us. In everything, and with everything.

• • •

LK   Where Thought Process is the field on which you build your philosophy, it seems to me that Meditation is the cornerstone for the edifice of that philosophy put into practice. Could you give us some of your thoughts as to why this is so?

FM   Yes, I would like to talk a little about creative Meditation. There are all kinds of Meditation, of course, volumes and volumes have been written on Meditation—the approach; the things to do; and the things not to do. What I'd I like to share here are the very basic terms of Meditation:

1st) that one should be relaxed, with their eyes closed or opened;

2nd) that one should do some type of deep breathing.

3rd) that one should do this at the same time and place every day.

· · ·

LK   Haven't you left out one of the basics of Meditation?

FM   No, I don't think so.

LK   I'm thinking of mantras. Aren't they basic to Meditation?

FM   People have often asked me about mantras, do we have to use a mantra, what sort of mantra is best, or what do I, myself, use as a mantra. But to answer your question, is a mantra necessary, or basic to Meditation, I would so no. No, because I think each of us needs to be creative to his or her own individuality, meaning that if we wish to create our own mantra, or if one comes to us, fine.
   Now in the case of using objects of envisioning for meditative purposes, my suggestion is the use of Color. Color is energy. And if we're properly in tune, or at least working toward that direction, we will be given, not by man, but by an Infinite Intelligence, the Color, or the Energy, that is appropriate to us at any given time in relationship to Meditation.

LK   In all the explanations and methods of Meditation that I've encountered, I've never found any stress on the exact time and place as being necessary to Meditation. Why is it that you stress the same place and time?

FM   Because if we are willing to take that same time each day, in the same place, we will build up an energy and a resource whereby there are other energies that can come in and interplay with ours. Energies that can help us, or guide us, or direct us in certain ways with our needs.

LK   Could you be more specific as to what these energies are?

FM   No, I can't really be specific.

LK   Really? I've been under the impression that in Meditation we are working with entities, or persons from the other side, usually loved ones that have proceeded us to the life beyond this life.

FM   That's right. That's exactly what I mean by energies that can help us, or guide us, in whatever. The energies directed by persons on the other side who care for us.

LK   Then in saying that you can't be specific, you are saying that you can't be specific about how the energies work that come from those concerned persons?

FM   Yes. That was my meaning.

LK   What if the same place or time is not possible, such as when you are traveling, or when there are other interruptions in your time and space?

FM   In that case, you send out a thought to the effect that you will not be at your usual time or place. It is a courtesy to those who work with you. It's like saying `call me on the phone at such and such a time,' and if you're not there ... well, you're not there. There's no contact.

LK   These persons, or entities, who work with us during Meditation, can they follow us and find us if we are moving about? Especially if we let them know approximately where we will be at an approximate time.

FM   Yes.

LK   Going back, now, to the basics of Meditation, and I realize that you want to keep your comments on Meditation as simple as possible, but would you elaborate on the above three principles a little further?

FM   Certainly.

• • •

    1)   I would suggest sitting or lying down;

    2)   the eyes can be open or closed, preferably closed, because once the eyes are closed it is easer to create your atmosphere.

By atmosphere, I mean the creation of a Light of good all around yourself. Imagine this, so that you feel a sense of well-being, a feeling that you are, in fact, encompassed by the warmth of this Light and Power. It doesn't have to be with any words. It's just a sense, a kind of feeling;

    3)   use a candle, if you wish, or create an altar, or music, if you feel comfortable with that;

    4)   make your place of Meditation a place that only you, for the most part, occupy. This is so that the vibrations will be yours, and yours alone;

    5)   once in position and comfortable, the next step is breathing. I would recommend step breathing. By step breathing, I mean, breathing to a count of one, two, and three. That is 1st, the expanding of the upper chest; 2nd, the filling up of the lungs down mid-way, and 3rd, the filling of the lower lungs so that your

abdomen expands. Babies, you will notice, do this naturally, and it is most easily, or naturally, achieved when lying on one's back.

6) The next step, of course, is to exhale in the same manner, a reversal of the above process, also to a count of three. In other words, you breathe in and you breathe out.

Now when you breathe in you may wish to envision the taking in of all that is good for your being, and when breathing out envision the releasement of the toxins, limitations, doubts, or any fears you have;

7) do this for two or three minutes, and just make it comfortable. Everything we want to do in relationship to Meditation we want to do it in a comfortable manner. Breath is truly the breath of life simply because without it, as we know, nothing works.

8) The full mediation should take about twenty minutes.

9) And as I have already said, it is important to work with Meditation on a daily basis, at the same time and at the same place. Obviously, there will be exceptions to the rule. Again, I stress that on these occasions you should remember to send out a thought that you are unable to be there at your appointed time. You do this as a courtesy to those who may be working with you.

10) As far as mantras go, I believe that over a period of time, through practice, you will begin to create your own rituals of Meditation. Life is creative, and although we like to have, even need to have, certain things to follow, certain rules and rituals to work with at first, there comes a time when we begin to maneuver and apply our own intuitive processes according to where we are coming from.

11) And finally, I recommend the morning, as morning is the best time to meditate, only because we are more alert than in the evening, we might even fall asleep during the evening.

• • •

Another approach to Meditation is to use the same steps as above, but I'd advise in this case lying down on the floor or on a bed looking up to the ceiling and visualizing the third eye, the Spiritual Eye, which is between the two eyes on the forehead.

Think of projecting Energy from this third eye as if it were a flashlight. Imagine the Light from the third eye broadening as it extends to the ceiling. This may be quite difficult at first, though with practice you will be successful.

• • •

I'd also like to point out that in our first experiences with Meditation, we usually find that all kinds of things enter our minds: thoughts, pictures, words, whatever. But as we continue this practice we will find that we are stilling the mind to a point where we will have gone beyond all this commotion into true silence. We will enter into what we might call a dream state. The only thing I can say about this place of silence is that it is very, very special and very wonderful. That in this silence there is no fear, or doubt, or whatever else we may have conjured up and created in our lives.

It is up to us, through practice, how long it will take to achieve a truly powerful Meditation—days, months, years—time is not a concern of Spirituality. It is our well being and the feeling that we share with those with whom we surround ourselves that will be the real net result.

• • •

LK   What would you say is the single most important thing to remember to do during Meditation?

FM   The most important thing of all in Meditation is to relax.

LK   Both physically and mentally?

FM   Yes. Especially to become as quiet of mind as possible, but without strain. Deep breathing can facilitate this.

LK   And the physical will follow?

FM   Or the other way around. Simply relax.

LK   Have you anything else to add to the understanding of basic Meditation?

FM   I would like to say, here, that there is a difference between Prayer and Meditation. This is an important distinction. Meditation is something that we are a part of, prayer is usually meant as a petition to a Source. That is to say, that in prayer we are usually asking for something. Whereas in Meditation we are released from the asking. We know that the Infinite is already here and that we already have what we need. And so there is a difference between Meditation and Prayer. Both are good. Both receive results.

LK   There's one other thing, I think belongs with this section on Meditation and that is the nature of Concentration. Until recently I had thought that Visualization and Concentration where interchangeable words for the same process. I didn't realize there was a difference.

FM   But you recognize there is a difference now?

LK   Yes.

FM   What makes you feel there's a difference now? And what is that difference in your mind?

LK   Well, the other day when we were talking off the tape about Meditation, you said something to the effect that Concentration was just the opposite of Meditation. And from that I concluded that both Meditation and Concentration at their best are . . . well, there's just nothing, no visual images, no verbal chatter, just emptiness and silence. At that point, I realized that what I have been calling Concentration is actually Visualization.
   Which brings me to the thought, right now, that one might start with visualization, or the asking of a question, but then one would just let that sort of . . . let their Concentration become so dense in that area that the actual question or image fades out of their consciousness.

FM   Exactly. You got it.

LK   Okay. So—

FM   It's similar to an example I've given many times, of how people will send out a thought for someone in need, and then they'll do it several times more in the course of the day. To me that means they've visualized, but they haven't really concentrated. Because if they had really concentrated on that name, that condition, that situation, they would have a sense within their own being that, `It's not necessary to send out another thought. I've done everything I can. And that's it.' With Concentration, you do it once, you're confident, and that's it.

You see, everything we do in the Spiritual field takes a lot of Concentration, because here on Earth we are surrounded with negation, and we have to get through that. It's like peeling an onion. It takes a great amount of energy to peel away all the layers of negation to reach the heart of the situation we wish to effect. Visualization is kind of like saying, `Oh, I visualized it, but I'm not putting much energy into it.' We have to put a concentrated amount of energy into it.

LK   And that would also be true of a truly effective prayer?

FM   Yes.

LK   In effect you are saying that since our High Self, our In-dwelling God, knows what we are after, we don't really have to say or visualization anything. It's like saying to the In-dwelling God, or High Self, "This period of Concentration is to build Energy for you know what."

FM   Exactly. It's just like talking to another person. But you then have to be in a state of mind in which there is nothing else. Nothing else.

LK   Now auto-suggestion, by which I mean self-hypnosis, would be much the same as visualization, and a good place to start, but you would have to go further into true Concentration for best results?

FM   Right. To me, auto-suggestion or visualization, are separate in essences, simply because in visualization, or auto-suggestion, we are not necessarily giving the situation we wish to effect a total Energy. With Concentration there is such a strong demand for the specific thought that nothing else takes precedence. Whereas, to me, in visualization our energies often times waffle. Concentration is more centered.

LK   So you might start by visualizing—

FM   Yes, you might begin with visualization, but then you secure the post, so to speak.

LK   Basically speaking then, to bring about an effective Concentration, you breath deeply, relax, and talk to yourself intelligently. Maybe select out of your past experiences only those that are good, those that will reinforce the sense of confidence you now want, and then you become so focused on this one specific area of concern, that you will experience a blankness, or a nothingness, the same as in the best moments of Meditation.

FM   That about sums it up.

LK   For the reader's benefit, perhaps I should explain here, that when we speak of the High Self, the Middle Self, the Low Self, we are referring to the Triune concept of Self, which, roughly speaking, consists of, one, a High Self, which might be thought of as the source of our intuitive qualities; two, a Middle Self, which is our conscious mind; and, three, a Low Self, which is the power supply that runs the body, stores the memories, builds the emotions and so on.

FM   Roughly speaking.

LK   Now when we appeal to God for guidance, or super human strengths of mind or body for Healing and other miracles, we are appealing to the High Self, our In-dwelling God.

FM   Correct.

LK   I think it would be useful to go into more detail about this Triune Self concept and its potential use as a working outline for Concentration, but first, I would like to talk with you some more about Fare-Thee-Well, the Healing Center that you, along with others, founded in 1974.

FM   Fine.

PART THREE
How Fare-Thee-Well Came to be and What Was Its Nature

LK   At the end of Part One, we left you standing in the pulpit at the First Congregational Church of Huntington, Massachusetts, spontaneously telling your congregation that you were leaving, resigning from your position of minister to that congregation and church. At that time you had been minister to that particular church for five years. Was this spontaneous resignation totally "unbeknownst" to you?   Was there nothing leading up to it that might have given you a clue if you had noticed?

FM   No.

LK   In looking back could you put your finger on a specific incident or reason?

FM   To answer that, I'd like to go back a few years to the beginning of my ministry at the First Congregational Church in Huntington. As I have told you, I was encouraged by the minister that had married me and my wife to become a lay minister in the United Church of Christ, which I did. And that after some three years of filling a pulpit here and there, a position came open for a part-time minister but full time on Sundays at the Congregational Church over in Huntington, and I took it, because I didn't feel I could get across fully the message I wanted to share, just being at any particular church for only one Sunday at a time.

   I suppose you could say that Fare-Thee-Well began at the little church in Huntington, when I was asked to start an evening

Bible class.

Now I didn't really want to call this study group a Bible class, because I never thought of my teachings as religious, rather as Spiritual or philosophical. So I preferred to use the name Spiritual Awareness class. Most of the group were comfortable with this approach to Spiritual Awareness, but there were those who dropped out when they saw that these teachings would include paranormal phenomena, reincarnation, psychic healing and other such happenings. But for those who stayed, it became an interesting experience. A lot of people had a lot of things happening in Meditation and Concentration at that time.

There was one particular evening when one of the women in our gathering spoke of a particular woman. She described this woman; and then another member of our group gave the name of this woman described; and still another of our group told what this woman did. The woman that they were "picking up on" was a nun who worked with Healing, and it all kind of dovetailed from there.

LK   You are referring to an unseen presence, I take it?

FM   Yes. Another evening, I described a piece of land. I had no notion of where it was, but I described it. I perceived it like a topographical map, an aerial view of this piece of property.

That same evening, after the meeting, one of the couples in our group asked if we wanted to have a picnic after church next Sunday, and we all said sure. So on Sunday we had our picnic on a piece of land they owned nearby. And as we were going onto this piece of property, I could see more and more that this was the place I had described the week before. It was about twenty or twenty-two acres of land overlooking the hillside to the mountains. It was very beautiful.

• • •

And so we continued our Spiritual Awareness services at the church in Huntington. Then one Sunday, the people that owned the land on which we had had our picnic, said that if we wanted to have our Spiritual Awareness services on that property they would donate the land. Of course, they didn't donate the land to me, they donated it to this group. Which was fine.

By mid-August I had left the church in Huntington, and we were having meetings over in the field, which was really great. Since we didn't have any structure, we didn't have anything to raise funds for, or whatever. Those were very special Sundays.

And then, of course, the weather started to get colder, and so there was a couple in the group whose home was nearby, and they said, "Well, why don't we meet at our place." It was about six people that were meeting at that time. And so we went over to their house, and we met there.

The number of people, by word of mouth I guess, started to grow and we were having anywhere between twenty to fifty people on Sunday mornings at the home of these people.

It really wasn't right or fair to them, as they had four children and it was a disruptive thing on a Sunday. And so some of the group suggested that we needed some kind of place, some kind of structure at which to gather. I agreed. We needed some kind of structure.

So they started talking about it, and looking into it, and finally found that if we were going to have a structure, the state would have a lot to say about what kind of structure. Are you going to live in it? No. Are you going to make money? Well yes, probably we'll take in money to do this or that. And how's it going to be done? Is it going to be non-profit, or religious, and so forth?

The people decided to do it as a religious venture. I, personally, didn't think too much of that direction, because I never thought of my teachings as religious, rather as Spiritual or philosophical. But I was only one of many at the time, and so that was how and why it went through as a religious situation.

The state said it would probably take three to four years to put our papers through, but it just happened that I knew the woman who was secretary to the Secretary of State in Massachusetts. And this women okayed most of the things that the Secretary of State would sign. And so, she put through our papers, and we had it within a month's time. We were an official organized religion. That was the last way I wanted to see it happen, but nevertheless it did.

Then they started to build the church in, or rather the structure, in the Spring. At the time when I had described the land at the Awareness Class, I had also described the structure. So they built the structure in accordance to the way I had described it. Now some of the specifications which I had described at that time had no logical reason for being, nonetheless, it was built as I had first described it.

And as time went on, you could see why we had windows high up on one side, low on another, because of different things we would have reasons for on the wall space. We had it lower on the south side, and so forth. All these details in the plan of the structure were in direct connection with intuitive, or Spiritual guidance, I believe.

And when it came to a question of water, it was a similar process. We didn't have a surface well or any other naturally existing water supply. Everyone felt that we should be involved in getting water, and I agreed.

They had three different dowsers come to the property to check for water. But one Sunday morning, while I was talking to the group outside, I heard a bird nearby, and I suggested that that was were the water should be drilled for. It wasn't anywhere near the place that the three dowsers had agreed upon as the best place to drill for water. Nonetheless, the group did drill where I had suggested to drill and they received a tremendous amount of water.

In that whole area, which is called Norwich Hill, people had gone down hundreds of feet and gotten very little water. The church where all this had begun, was only about two miles from where our structure was being built. And there, at the church, they had gone over two hundred feet to find water and after twenty minutes of washing dishes they would run out of water for a day. And here we had an amazing fifteen gallons a minute, an ample supply.

And this was the way we did things at Fare-Thee-Well. A kind of knowing and a guiding way. I became ordained through that group, through that congregation. I was their minister, and I was also their Spiritual Leader, as well as their President.

From that point on, we had many different classes. Such things as life after death, reincarnation, how to handle daily living, and so forth.

LK   How did you arrive at the name for this Wholeness Center?

FM   At the time when all this activity was going on, one of the members in the group received a mental picture of a sign that read "FARE-THEE-WELL". I don't think any of us were sure what the phrase meant because we had to look it up in a dictionary, where we found that the word meant "a state of perfection." This certainly was what we were after, so we called our new organization by that name, and when the time came to deed the land over to this newly formed Spiritual Community it was deeded over to Fare-Thee-Well.

LK   In preparing for this interview, I read an account of those early days of Fare-Thee-Well. There seemed to be a high energy of enthusiasm and sense of community in the written account. I recall reading that everyone pitched in to clear the area, cut trees and brush to prepare for a road to be bulldozed, and that in the evenings there would be a meal and everyone would sit around a fire and sing songs after a hard day of work.

FM   Yes, it was a wonderful time of working together, of community spirit and Spiritual development.

LK   I also recall that there was not one project started for which the financial needs were not met, often from unexpected sources, which enhanced the belief of that group (a belief I, myself, share and will touch on in a later section), that all of their needs would be met.

FM   Yes, that's true.

LK   Besides teaching your method of Healing through Light, Color, and the awareness of the perfect energies that are always present, you, as well as others of the Fare-Thee-Well members, were open to a variety of wholistic health practices. Is that correct?

FM   Yes. I wanted to keep it as free as possible. For example, one of the things we did, in relationship to Healing, was herbs. My wife was involved, and is involved, with herbs in regards to the beauty of them, as well as their medicinal purposes, so that became one of the practices of Healing used in certain instances. We also stressed the use of natural foods.

LK   Also there was a good-sized library of books on Healing, Spiritual development, and the paranormal in general, as I recall. Are there any other activities or features at Fare-Thee-Well during those early years, that you would care to mention before we move on?

FM   I think that about covers it.

LK   Good. In the next section, I will present, as you have already suggested, some essays about the Fare-Thee-Well experience of the 1980's that were published in "Country Journal," a local newspaper serving the hill towns in and around Huntington, Massachusetts at that time, after which I would like to explore your thoughts and ideas on Spiritual Communities today, some twenty years since the founding Fare-Thee-Well.

PART FOUR
Introduction to the Essays Printed in
"Country Journal," 1983-84

In 1983, COUNTRY JOURNAL, a newspaper then serving the hill towns of southwestern Massachusetts, where Fare-Thee-Well was located, began a weekly column call "Pastor's Corner." I had been attending services and classes at Fare-Thee-Well for about two years at that time, and was asked, along with others, by Floyd, if I would share some of my experiences at Fare-Thee-Well in this column, which I did. I wrote, however, not as a "pastor", which I am not, but, clearly stated, as a member of Fare-Thee-Well.

During the preparation of the manuscript for "A Kind of Knowing," Floyd suggested that we might use some of those essays to give an idea of the Thought Process he was teaching at that time. I agreed not only to show what I was getting out of Fare-Thee-Well at that time, but also because that is where I came into the picture.

At the time of writing these essays, I used a quasi-traditional Christian and New Age language. It had its reasons at the time, and so I have left the essays as they were originally written, though I would now want to write with a fresh language, a pragmatic language, one not over-laden with connotations.

The reason for this is that words such a "Love," "Death," "God," "Spirit," "Soul," and so forth, have come to mean so many different things from years of use and "misuse," that one almost has to define these words anew each time they are used, and also, because I am not so much talking of commandments, morals, or religious precepts, as I am talking of principles. Those laws which are. Both the laws of physics, and the laws of thought.

For example: God. What does it bring to mind? A large

anthropomorphic male being with a flowing white beard, most likely. And having come that far, it is easy to imagine Him meting out rewards and punishments. I know I did.

But as I came into adulthood this was not a satisfactory concept. It didn't fit with certain experiences I was having, and there was a time of emptiness then chaos before need demanded a new image. This new image took the form of a vast amoeba that surrounded the stars. An Energy, an Intelligence, a Substance, which included everything, with everything immersed in it and made of it, as a fish is in the ocean and the ocean is in the fish. The fish being, in short, a clotted thought within the mind of the ocean, and the ocean, here, being both the field spoken of in quantum physics and the Oneness experienced by the Eastern mystic. A poetic view which, I hope, is accurate to the Universe of both the mystic and the quantum physicist. If not, still a personal mind-picture of the One Intelligence, Energy, and Substance which is the Universe.

There are times, however, when one needs something more personal. Something different from the medieval God, as anthropomorphic being, yet something warmer than an existential abstracted deity.

The In-dwelling God; the Christ consciousness; the High Self; the Father; the Over Soul; the Mother and Father Self (that absolutely dependable parent-self of the Kahunas), are to me synonymous, but I prefer some over others because of the meaning I have given them. I might also have found my image in something I find benevolent in nature.

The many faces of Shiva-Shakti, the personified god-goddess (Brahma) of Hinduism, is a beautiful image of the impersonal supreme being, the primal source and ultimate goal of all beings, with which Atman, or the individual self, knows itself to be identical, when enlightened. But here I am afraid of getting back to God by the way of gods.

Whatever image you use, I believe it should be a personal creation, as each of us must ultimately create his or her own images and rituals for the process of drawing upon The One Power.

And just so the Devil may not be missing from this book, I will say this. So far as I am concerned, there is no Satan, except as a symbol of man's ignorance. I have never met the Devil or any devil. All the trouble I have gotten myself into, I did out of choice. I knew what I was doing, or at least did it willfully, though sometimes I was so ignorant within that wilifulness that I would have been happy to say, "The Devil made me do it." But I feel that I have always known better than that, and can honestly say that I have never felt "tempted" by any source outside my own psyche. In saying that I have no knowledge of any devil, I am echoing Mr. McAuslan, from whom I first caught the glint of this concept.

As I have said, at the time of the writing of these essays, I used a quasi-traditional Christian and New Age language, and having willingly done so, I will own them as first published, and as still being Truth principles in my experience. Principles by another other name, the same.

. . .

- 2 -
Essay 1
"Notes Toward Spiritual Virtuosity"
(Country Journal, Huntington, Massachusetts, Thursday, February 17, 1983)

To be "in tune" is an often-heard phrase at The Healing Center at Fare-Thee-Well. To the members of this Spiritual Community, it means simply, a perfect state of balance between Mind, Body, and Spirit, a balance necessary for effective Healing.

For me, the words "in tune" also echo an experience I had as a trombone student at Oberlin Conservatory some years back. An experience that very nicely demonstrates one small facet of the greater Fare-Thee-Well experience.

Although I had given my all to the trombone, by my junior year, I was so bogged down in the concerns of technique that it looked as if I would never give my senior recital, let alone make fame and fortune for myself as a musician.

Being bogged down with technique meant that I was so concerned with doing it "right," so worried about embouchure, breath support, tonguing, etc., that I had severely crippled myself as a musician. The music was completely lost. It had become more important to produce a sound, any sound, the right way, then to produce the right sound, anyway.

When I returned to Oberlin after a summer away from the horn, I had a new approach. I told myself that I would just listen for the music until it sounded right, and not care any longer whether the technique used was the approved one or not. It worked. Two semesters later, I gave a passable recital and earned my Bachelor of Music degree.

Twenty years later, I came to Fare-Thee-Well with my life in a state of disharmony. Again, I had forgotten to "listen to the music."

As with my concern over technique on the trombone, one of my problems when I first met the Reverend Floyd McAuslan, founder of Fare-Thee-Well, was that I was trying to control my life by intellect alone. This is not to disparage the intellect, but there comes a time to "listen to the music," the inner-self, or the God-within.

With the intellect we make a decision, say, based on an examination of the facts. To worry that decision once it has been made is to frustrate the inner-self in its efforts to implement that decision. In other words, you make the decision (you learn the technique), and then you "listen for the music." The inner-self will know the score, will know how to interpret the needs of the conscious mind.

To assist in hearing this music, Reverend McAuslan has provided five principles for Fare-Thee-Well. They are a belief in Infinite Intelligence as an ever present Power; eternal life for all; that true growth of oneself comes when it is shared in helping all life in mind, spirit, and body; daily attunement to draw closer to the perfection of God's creation of Love, Peace, Joy, Harmony, and Truth; and that Perfection always has been and always will be.

I would like to add, that practice makes perfect, or, if you like, persistence makes a fare-thee-well: that is, "a state-of-perfection," or should I say, Fare-Thee-Well, a state of in-tunement.

. . .

- 3 -
Essay 2
"Thoughts Toward Peace"
(Country Journal, Huntington, Massachusetts, Thursday, February 2, 1984)

This second essay, "Thoughts Toward Peace," I believe to be based on one of the most fundamental principles which were taught by Reverend McAuslan at Fare-Thee-Well. A principle that can also be applied to the environmental concerns of our time, or for that matter, to all and any of the happenings that result from our collective consciousness. And please note, and as one reader did, politics are never mentioned. It is that universal a principle, and as far as this interviewer and author of the following essay is concerned, the opening sentence, the very next sentence you read, says it all.

. . .

All things proceed from thought. Before any art, before any business, before any community can be realized in space and time it must first be known in thought. If we would desire world peace, then conceive world peace, see world peace in thought.

And we must love peace rather than hate war. For if all things proceed from thought (and they do) and we hate war, we are thinking hate—that combustible energy from which war flares up. Each time we think hate we are putting a splinter of kindling on the pyre of world holocaust.

To fight fire with fire is not the analogy for world peace. One can hardly imagine a Gandhi or a Schweitzer marching to such a slogan. Rather we must substitute for each splinter of hate a fiber of love, the asbestos of lasting peace. For if all things proceed from thought (and they do) and the many of us each holds firm to the thoughts of peace, then, in time, the pastures of peace will green over the barren fields of battle.

All things proceed from thought. Had Michelangelo approached the Sistine Chapel with satanic thoughts we would not have that great image of God giving life to Adam.

Had the Wright Brothers not believed in flight, their first aircraft would have become a collection of splinters and torn linen on the sands of Kitty Hawk.

Had Henry Ford been unable to see his assembly line from start to finish it would have broken down in those blind spots in his thought and left him just another dreamer, as opposed to a man of vision.

It is well recognized that all great men of vision have the ability, regardless of negative distracters, to persist in their vision. That is the straight and narrow, the adherence to a positive vision of life. Belief is persistence. Faith is persistence. Faith without persistence is dead.

Mickey Mouse, the Howard Johnson chain, and the

democracy which is the United States of America were all first a thought. First the thought of an individual and then the thought of many individuals, making the collective thought of a corporation or a people. And these institutions will hold as long as there is sufficient belief in their validity and to the extent of that belief.

The Roman Empire and the Third Reich were the same. First a thought, then an actuality. Now an actuality from which the belief has gone.

Good and evil are but the realities of positive or negative thought. Our thought, through universal law, is built for us according to the strength (individual or collective) of our belief in that thought, whether they are plus or minus.

A knife is neither good nor evil. It is the thought we bring to it that makes it a tool or a weapon. And so it is that we must love peace, rather than hate war.

All things proceed from thought, and mystics tell us to spend time each day in visualizing our needs, and promise that these needs, first created in thought, will be met by us in time and space. An attitude supportive to these visualizations must be maintained the rest of the day, however, or their original vigor is lessened.

It is obvious, in the examples above, that the Wright Brothers; that Henry Ford; that the founding fathers of our American democracy, held uppermost in their minds the belief in their objectives. They did not waver. They held the future ever present in their minds. They walked the straight and narrow of positive thought. And they realized their dreams.

It is the same in our daily lives. If we view our lives as dull or burdensome, then they are dull or burdensome. If we view our lives as a challenge and an adventure, then they are a challenge and an adventure. That is the only difference between the successful and the unsuccessful of this earth. Their viewpoint, their thought, the way in which they elect to see their lives.

And it is the same with the collective thoughts of the race. It is a troubled world or it is a pasture of peace and contentment, all according to our collective viewpoint. If we seek war we will find war. If we seek peace we will find peace. How could it be otherwise? Nature does not make war, only we make war.

All things proceed from thought, and if we insist on images of world holocaust, holocaust becomes inevitable.

If some of us, enough of us, insist on images of peace, of overcoming the current tensions on our planet that have arisen out of our collective negativity, we can offset a world holocaust. If enough of us, if all of us, hold images of peace and feelings of brotherly love and Spiritual unity in our thoughts we can not only offset world holocaust, but create world peace. Where there is the greater concentration of thought there will be our reality. For this reason we must love peace, rather than hate war. For hate is war, whatever its guise.

This is not a new message. We have heard it before. It needs to be said again and often as we approach the climax of a long epoch of contention. An approach and a climax that we ourselves are programming.

This situation we have created ourselves. It certainly would not exist without us, and we are not any of us islands. We have all participated. To see it otherwise is to shirk our responsibility to ourselves and our neighbors. Though it may be hard to see how we as individuals can be that responsible, we must learn to do so.

We are, each of us, like a cell in our body. If one cell gets sick it threatens another, and if two cells become sick then three or four are affected, and so on, until illness, a cancer, say, threatens the whole organism. The ocean is made of drops of water.

We cannot blame leaders. Leaders, both in democracies and in dictatorships, are only representatives of group consciousness, for they, too, have been molded by the Thought Process of the society of which they are a part.

All things proceed from thought, and the fearsome auguries

of our age are our own. As we learn in our private lives that we must ultimately take responsibility for ourselves if we are to partake of the universal laws for happiness and success, so it would seem that we must take responsibility for ourselves as a race if we would have those same laws of the universe work for us as a unit. It is unlikely that any benevolent beings will descend from the dark of space to bail us out of a dilemma of our own making.

Since all things proceed from thought, the absolute control of our destiny is our own by the focus of our thought, now, in the present moment. Will it be plus or minus? Hate or love? War or peace?

The answer, the reality of tomorrow, is precisely what you think it is.

• • •

- 4 -
Essay 3
"Consider The Lilies"
(Country Journal, Huntington, Massachusetts, Thursday, June 23, 1983)

This third essay was of special importance to me at the time of its composition and touches on another of the bottom line principles taught by Reverend McAuslan at Fare-Thee-Well. I wish to make it clear to you, the reader, that when I used the maxim, "Letting go and letting God," I did not, and still do not, mean to imply in any way, that we just sit back and do nothing. Releasement is not passivity, but rather an active process of Will.

• • •

Releasement, or "Letting go and letting God," is the technique of letting go of the fear, or the worry, that so often frustrates our efforts toward a desired result.

Last winter I found releasement to be the prescription needed to heal an unemployment dis-ease I had contracted.

I had discussed releasement and my unemployment with the Reverend Floyd McAuslan at the Healing Center at Fare-Thee-Well during this time. The concepts that I applied toward Healing that unemployment dis-ease are greatly my own, but I think that is largely the intent of Fare-Thee-Well: to help individuals find the answers they need within themselves.

Basically I have concluded from last winter's experience that "so long as you are willing to put one foot in front of the other, the universe will meet your needs."

In other words releasement is more than just giving up the worry that frustrates your desired ends, it is also doing your part in making them happen, but without the worry, the frustration, and the fear. It is taking one step at a time and knowing you will get there because that is universal law.

In my particular case, Mr. McAuslan, recommended that I generate about a full week of work even though there seemed to be no immediate chance of financial return. He explained that any Energy we give out returns to us in some form, and that further, our needs are always met unless we ourselves block them through any of a number of disharmonies within ourselves.

I began the work immediately, but the releasement of anxiety over finances did not come so quickly. Releasement, I found, took an absolute confidence, or belief, like learning to float on one's back. You believe it can be done, yes, that the water will support you, certainly, but there is a moment when you must finally relax and let it happen. Before that you didn't believe.

For me that moment of trust came one starry November night as I took my anxiety out for yet another of our many walks. As I walked I realized that I was powerless to help myself and, in short, I became desperate. At that point releasement was simple. As simple as saying, "you handle it, I can't," and meaning it. I didn't know how it would happen, but I knew that everything would be okay.

That last part was like flipping a switch in a dark room and knowing that the light would appear, but not knowing anything of the technology that would make it appear. This, I think, is a lot of what we mean by faith.

At the moment that I released my fear the Healing was effective. I relaxed, my anxiety quieted, and within three days I had tangible results. I received a call offering work, the first of a series of freelance jobs that are becoming a full time service that I can offer in a field I enjoy.

I stress, however, that desperation is not necessary to releasement. It can be effected anytime, anywhere.

Although this experience has filled me with a book-full of things to share, for the space of this brief article I wish to convey only that so long as you are willing to put one foot in front of the other (invest Energy) and trust to the capabilities of the universe (releasement) your needs will be met, whatever they are.

An important catalyst in my own releasement prescription of last winter was Matthew 6: 25-34.

• • •

As I mentioned in the introduction to this book, there was a beautiful calligraphy on the wall at Fare-Thee-Well of the five principles that Mr. McAuslan had put down as a foundation for that group. Although they are listed in the first essay "Notes Toward Spiritual Virtuosity," I would like to conclude this segment by listing them as a concise statement of what Fare-Thee-Well was all about.

The Five Principles Used at Fare-Thee-Well:

1) Infinite Intelligence.

2) Eternal life.

3) True growth comes about in the sharing and helping of all life in mind, spirit, and body.

4) Daily attunement to draw closer to the perfection of God's creation. Love, Peace, Joy, Harmony, and Truth.

5) Perfection always has been and always will be.

PART FIVE
Thoughts on a Spiritual Community

LK   What was the purpose of Fare-Thee-Well as you saw it in its original conception?   What are your thoughts on a Spiritual Community?

FM   I think a Spiritual Community is a wonderful way to grow. I think we've planted ourselves here on Earth for the growth process. Originally, it seems to me, mankind got off to a poor start, that is to say we got involved in the survival of the fittest, and I think we haven't grown too far from that at this particular point in time. It's still a first me then you can be second kind of attitude.

In a Spiritual Community, I believe you have to have a common denominator, which would be a desire for growth. Now that doesn't mean that the community needs to be rigid, it doesn't mean that the community cannot be versatile, by any means.

The main object of having a Spiritual Community, or being a part of a Spiritual Community, is the daily practice of awareness. That is an awareness of the Spiritual faculties, not only of one's self but of those that we're surrounded by.   And it must be practiced on a daily basis. That doesn't mean that it needs to be a long period of time each day. Perhaps no more than half hour, once or twice a day. Maybe once a day at meal time. But it must be on a daily basis for it to be effective and it must be done together, and it must be a community affair of working together in varied ways.

For example, if you're going to have an organic garden, or if you are going to be building homes, or if you are going to be snow plowing, you would have, for the economics involved, each person chipping in a certain amount of money for the snow plow, or giving a certain amount of his or her time for the care of the garden, or a certain amount of labor for the building of the homes.

Now this isn't trying to build something separate from the town or the state. This is a part of this particular Spiritual Community. You see, we build from Energy and this Energy will build accordingly through thought, the quality of that thought and the intensity of that thought.

Now there is going to be pain at first from this group gathering, this group's collective consciousness, simply because we're not familiar with it. If we have an arm that just hangs down for six months and we try to lift it up, it won't go, or if it does, it will go very little, because it is not familiar with the movement. In other words, if we're not familiar with something we find it very difficult to do. That's why we need the common denominator of a desire for Spiritual growth to unify us.

It doesn't mean we need to stay on the land for survival, or livelihood. It means we go out into the world and do our daily tasks of earning a living and so forth. We are not an island unto ourselves. We need to be flexible. We need to be in the world.

The largest thing is the growth and, if you will, the pain, which simply comes about because of the change. But as time moves on, if one is willing to stick with it, it will be very special and very beautiful. However, because of the economics of our times, it is not a feasible direction in which to go. I believe, however, that we are at the threshold of great change.

Of course, as a race we have often been through times of great change. From the outset of the industrial age in the 1800's until now we have seen much changed. But along with our accelerated progress in technology a lack of enough time for the family has somehow occurred. Families are stripped today. In the context of the family unit, the separation is greater today than perhaps at any time in history.

We're going to have to learn how to grow back to that unity, learn again to understand and comprehend the unification, because we are all made of the same putty, we are all put together in that same manner. We need one another, and yet our concept of survival is separating our consciousness more and more from this community of thought.

The advantage of a community is to be strong, to help us wax strong in all aspects of our lives, so that we are able to help not only the immediate community but the outer community as well. By unifying first the family and then the extended family of a Spiritual Community, we are gluing together, and building on, and strengthening the unlimited Spiritual resources of each individual's divinity, and therefore, that small group's emanations of Spiritually-oriented thought spreads out into the thinking of the entire population on the planet Earth and is manifest in many ways. Ways that perhaps we do not see nor will ever comprehend, but there is that strengthening process.

And so the greatest time to build a community is the time when there is great turmoil. But that is also the most difficult time to create, because we find that we need, or seem to need, to separate ourselves to survive, when, in fact, it is through the unity of the many that we have the qualifications to survive. And for that we need the Spiritual gatherings to unify the understanding of what is needed.

LK So on one hand we have the community, on the other, the hermit. Doesn't the hermit-sage have a place? Doesn't he, through his solitary Spiritual practices development himself for the many?

FM Yes, that right. He's being totally creative. He has to survive and be sustained and so he's being creative. Anytime one is creative, they are touching the resources of the Infinite. And that's what life is all about. That's what any life is about. Being creative. You're in movement. You're not in stagnation.

A hermit that lives in the woods can be an unbelievably

Spiritual individual, because he or she, to survive, has had to be very, very creative. Also, I should make clear that in a community we are not so much dependent upon others, which is not bad, as we are being interdependent.

But when we have somebody do something for us, when we should be doing it ourselves, we are jeopardizing our consciousness, our thoughts, our life. We are what we are thinking, and if we are not thinking at all we're not very happy.

LK So on one hand, if you have a solitary coming into the community, he might find it extremely difficult—

FM Very.

LK —and others may find him extremely difficult.

FM Exactly.

LK But both are developing. Would this be one of the reasons that more than one lifetime is needed to get the balance between dependency and self-sufficiency?

FM That's right.

LK Would you say that for most individuals something a bit more toward the center, something between the extremes of community and aloneness is desirable?

FM As long as one is practicing a Spiritual Centering, it's good, it's marvelous. For instance, a person who doesn't believe in a Spiritual Source, a God, or whatever name you want to give it, but is a humanitarian, a good humanitarian, there is still a movement in the Spiritual progress. I have often found that to be the case. It's a different level. It's not higher or lower. I don't like to use the word level ...

LK   Frequency?

FM   Okay. It's a specific frequency that they are on and that, to my way of thinking, is still a Spiritual directive. Many people come to me as a healer, and say, "I'm an atheist, what can you do for me?" It's no big deal. They believe in something, they believe that they're atheists. It really doesn't make any difference. I don't care where anybody is coming from, or what their belief system is in regards to Healing, because where I'm coming from it makes no difference.

LK   This being an atheist. I can see it when your life is going well, or you're young enough to feel immortal, but I don't see how a person can have the courage to keep moving when by all earthly standards they've failed. Perhaps they continue just to leave things a little better for the generation coming along behind them, but even so, if you haven't any notion that what you are doing now is going to matter to you personally after you've gone, what keeps such an individual motivated toward growth?

FM   I don't know. I do know, however, that the people who really deteriorate the fastest are those who sit down and watch somebody else do something. It might be television, and they might say, `Hey, it's my turn to sit.' If they feel that way about their life, they've had it. It's time for them to move along, because they're just wasting their time.

· · ·

- 2 -
Essay 4
"Isn't It All `Jest For Pun'?"
(Country Journal, Huntington, Massachusetts, Thursday, February 16, 1984)

I intersperse here another of the essays written about the Fare-Thee-Well experience, in part, as a relief from the interview form and to some extent as a personality sketch of Mr. McAuslan, before we go into the heart of this book, Part Six: "The Practices of Healing." I would also like to add, that my use of the words "positive thought" throughout these essays, is not to be construed with false cheerfulness, or denying difficulties that do exist, or pretending to be happy when not. Rather it is the ideal of living intelligently, emphasizing the useful, the pragmatic, in short, those things that work in bringing about a posed mind and a harmonious relationship with all of life.

• • •

The Reverend Floyd McAuslan of Fare-Thee-Well in Huntington is the most "human" of metaphysicians I have ever met and always quick with a metaphor or a pun, whether in casual conversation or in teaching.

It was last spring that he likened the sparks from a campfire to the little thoughts of negativity that so often ignite our worries and our angers.

It was a daffodil morning with diamonds of dew still sparkling in the grass. We sat under the cherry tree in front of the drying shed that serves also as Fare-Thee-Well's Sunday morning meeting place in rough weather. We sat there listening to the robins and the honeybees and the Sunday morning talk by Floyd.

"When we sit around a bonfire," he said, "or a campfire and sparks alight on our clothing, a sleeve possibly, we flick it off automatically; we don't hesitate; we don't think about it; we don't consider the pros and cons; we flick it off without a second thought."

He said it should be the same when a spark of negativity alights on our consciousness; on the sleeve, the wool-gathering sleeve, I might add, of our consciousness. The Reverend McAuslan told us that we must be that quick; that automatic; that vigilant, if we are to learn the wealth and the wisdom of our spirits. After all, it is the disharmonies created by negative thinking that makes us ill at ease within our trinity of body, mind, and spirit.

He went on to liken the techniques of keeping a healthy, positive Thought Process to a diet. A diet of nothing but positive thought, he promised, would in time allow the Power of the spirit to build and to heal our every need just as we would expect a diet of wholesome and natural foods to build up the physical body.

He said, too, that like a diet for the body, it often took time before the cravings for negative thought were quelled and the diet of positive thought became the natural diet.

Of course, these metaphors are paraphrased from an already shifting memory. Recent enough in memory, however, not to need apology, is an exchange I had on the telephone with the Reverend McAuslan that illustrates some of the fun and play with words that make the serious business of Healing at Fare-Thee-Well the pleasurable business it should be.

I had called to question the reasons for a continuing discomfort I was having in an area on which I had been working for some months. I felt that progress had been made, yet various discomforts continued. Reverend McAuslan assured me that the sought-after progress had been made, and in explaining that I was experiencing only a certain amount of expected backlash said, "You're on the ship (meaning the ship of Healing and Growth), but you're not in the harbor yet." "I can easily believe that," I returned, "because I feel at sea all of the time." He laughed, and as I hung up the phone I felt on beam with port, once more.

Of the puns I promised none now come to mind, but among the many two-edged words of wit parried at Fare-Thee-Well you can be sure that prophet, sage, medium and thyme have played their part.

And though the Spiritual Path as taught by Reverend McAuslan at Fare-Thee-Well is a straight, or should I say, "strait" and narrow business, I have found the going lightened by the spontaneous; the "human"; the well phrased metaphor in teaching; as well as the extemporaneous "jest for pun."

PART SIX
The Practices of Healing

LK   Now, in the case of Healing, exactly how do you work? How do you approach a person who comes to you for help?

FM   In most instances of Healing, though not all, I work with Color. Color is a form of energy, and is a wonderful thing to acknowledge and experiment with. A good many years ago, I was given a Color by Fletcher, who was Arthur Ford's control, and I continue to use that same Color.
   To work with Color, I want to imbue myself with that Color. I want to be so filled with that Color that I no longer have any awareness of myself as an individual, or even any awareness of the dis-ease of the person that has come to me for help. It's not important to know what the dis-ease is, although most people like to share their particular problem, or name their sickness, which is fine.

LK   Could you tell a little about having no awareness of self? What is that like?

FM   If I am really in tune when I create my Color, I become immersed in this Color to a point that I may not be aware of who I am working with, even if I've known that person for a long time. I can't think of their name. I don't know my own name. I may be aware of other people in the room, but only as a sort of blur. I'm not in a trance state, however. I'm just there as a channel for this Energy, this particular Color that is working for the person who has come for Healing.

LK   When you say you're just a channel for Energy, or Color, working for the person, do you mean to say that the Color itself knows what to do for that individual, or do you mean that you are using this Color in a conscious way, and if so how do you know what to do with it?

FM   It is important to let the Light go in the directive that it desires to go. Not where we think it so should go, but where it wants to go. We are instruments, a channel as I've said, through which this Power works according to its own laws. In other words, it will manifest in its proper way for the situation at hand without any guidance from me. It is irrelevant what the dis-ease is, but totally relevant where and how the Power is working.

I'm saying that Color is an energy, an Infinite Energy of Intelligence. I think this is what God is, a Power and an Intelligence. In fact, you could say God is a Color, or rather all Colors, and that each of us understands and interprets this All-Color, this Power, this Energy, according to our level of consciousness and Spiritual growth. And as we grow Spiritually the Colors we use may change. No Color is good or bad. It is just a level of understanding.

LK   Sometimes you say "Color" and sometimes "Light." By Light do you mean the same thing as Color, a particular Color of Light?

FM   Quite often in the teaching of Healing, I use, as do many healers, the term "White Light." White Light is always appropriate, and can always be substituted for Color if no specific

Color comes to mind.

And again, I am saying that White Light is a Power of Infinite Intelligence. After all, what is more basic in Christian thought then to say, God is Light, God is Love. Love, also, being an Energy.

But in Healing, I have found it helpful to work with my specific Color, and so I recommend the use of a specific Color, or else White Light where no specific Color presents itself. I might mention, also, that a Color may remain constant or change from time to time. Over the years or during a Healing. This is nothing to be concerned about.

LK By "Light" do you always mean "White Light" when speaking of Spiritual matters?

FM I suppose I must use "Light" and "White Light" interchangeably. Yes.

LK To sum up what you've just said, then: Color, or White Light, is the most important thing to be aware of when Healing. That, and the directing of this Color, or White Light, to the individual in need of Healing.

FM Right. Though this is not to be confused with a trance, or a semi-consciousness state in any way. It is just that you are the Light, the Energy of this Light, and that you are directing this Light to the individual. That is a constructive method for the Healing of the individual.

LK When you say that you are the Light and when you say you are a channel for the Light, I take it that you mean the same thing?

FM Yes.

LK It seems to me that the condition you described a moment ago, of not knowing the name of the person who has come to you for Healing, or their illness, or even your own name, would be quite disturbing, even frightening.

FM At first it was. I'm used to it now, and I can remind myself that things will return to normal, and I'll know my name again, and who the person is that I've been working with.

• • •

LK In teaching a beginner the art of Healing, where do you begin, what do you recommend?

FM First I'd like deal with "Self-Healing." Just a simple, brief explanation, a list of a few simple steps, a few practices that I have found useful in most instances of Self-Healing.

LK All right. I'll present your comments here in the form of a numbered list.

Steps in Self-Healing By Color

1) On the day of the Healing, eat lightly, avoiding meat, no later than six hours before the scheduled time of Healing.

2) Take a hot shower just before the time of Healing. (This opens the pores and makes one more receptive to the energies you will be working with.)

3) Prepare yourself as you would for Meditation, using your usual place of Meditation, if possible. (See Part Two,

Meditation, pages 20 - 22.)

4) Choose a Color which may or may not be your favorite color. Let it be one that comes into your mind at that time.

5) Visualize the Color as filling your body, beginning with the top of your head. Work the Color down through the head to the face, the eyes, nose, mouth, lips, and cheeks. Continue this progression on down through the neck, shoulders, arms, and hands, extending the Color out through the fingertips. Do this slowly.

6) Next return to the neck and work the Color down through the chest, stomach, and abdomen. Continue this progression on down through the thighs, legs, ankles, and feet, extending the Color out through the toes.

7) Return once more to the neck and visualize the Color as moving down through the back and through the area of the buttocks. Continue this progression on down through the back of the legs, ankles, feet, and again, extend the Color out through the toes.

8) At this point, you should be immersed in the Color you have created.

9) At times there are points within the body where the Color will stop. This usually means that there is an obstruction in that area. In such a case, imagine the Color as going through or around this area. (In such instances, you may find that more than one Color comes into play. That is all right.)

10) In the case of an obstructed area, you may want to return to that area for further work. This is recommended, but not

mandatory.

11) If you do return to this obstructed area, work with it in this manner.

   a) Visualize the condition, give it a name and acknowledge it.

   b) Next, immerse yourself and the affected area in White Light or the Color Energy you are working with.

   c) Stay immersed in White Light or Color to the point that this Light or Color is you.

   d) Do this for about three to five minutes.

12) The entire Healing procedure should take about twenty minutes and can be repeated on a daily basis for seven days. You can do it beyond the seven days if necessary.

• • •

LK   Again, I would like to clarify this matter of Color versus White Light.

FM   I recommend a specific Color where there is a strong feeling for that Color, but White Light, or `Light' as I often say, is always appropriate.

LK   In other words, White Light is generic, Color is a specific brand of Light.

FM   That's one way of putting it.

. . .

LK   The Healing techniques that we have just discussed are for working with one's self. Now what about the Healing of an individual other than one's self?

FM   In the case or working with another person, that is to work on their behalf, you would most likely use the laying on of hands, while imbuing yourself with White Light or a Color suggested at that moment.
    Again you would want to be relaxed and let the Color flow through your arms and hands to this other individual. Usually this is accomplished by standing behind the subject, who is seated or standing, and placing your hands on their shoulders. Always remembering to let the Color take its own direction.

LK   Could letting the Color take its own direction result in an urge to place one's hands on an afflicted area, or other area, of the other person's body, rather than merely placing your hands on their shoulders?

FM   That is one of the possible directives you might experience.

LK   And how do you know when you are receiving such a directive as opposed to just having a notion of your own?

FM   As with all Spiritual practices, the same as with any skill, whether it is in sports or music or whatever, it comes down to practice.

LK   How do you know how long to work with an individual in this manner?

FM If you are really in tune, you will know. A rule of thumb might be about three to five minutes.

・・・

LK The laying on of hands is used, of course, when the person to be worked with is right in front of you. In the case of absent treatment, that is, the Healing of a person who is not right in front of you, but at a distance, what procedures do you use?

FM Again I'd like these procedures to be listed and numbered for clarity.

・・・

Steps in Absent Healing

1) Acknowledge the person's full name and where you feel they are located geographically.

2) Visualize that person, not with the dis-ease, but as a full- blown, perfect being in spirit.

3) Then see them as being surrounded with White Light or a specific Color.

4) Hold to this thought for approximately three to five minutes.

5) Do this only once a day. And know you have done what you can, and that help has been sent on the Wings of Healing. I repeat, do it once a day. Know that you have done it, and let it alone for the rest of that day.

LK   In other words, `Don't worry it.'

FM   Exactly.

LK   Would twice a day be alright in extreme situations? I mean a situation where a family member or a friend is in a hospital in critical condition, you wouldn't be hurting the person by having that much concern, would you?

FM   That's a good point. Extreme situations. Because in general terms, to me, you do what you need to do for that situation for that day and that's it. And if you do it again, it's like saying, `I didn't have enough confidence the first time.' By the same token, I understand what you're saying. If the concerned person is so upset . . . well, they just have to go through it again, just because . . .
     I should like to point out, however, that there are times when one is not totally aware of the Power, or totally immersed in Color, and yet there are results. Good results. Positive results. And I might add, that in true Healing that particular dis-ease should not, or rather does not return.

LK   Why do you need to acknowledge the person's full name and place of location? Wouldn't your knowing the person be enough?

FM   At a Healing Service you are working not only with this Total Intelligence and Energy, but also with the Guardian Angels of the person to be healed. To say Joe, Mary, Frank, or John is as vague to that person's Guardian Angels, their loved ones on the other side, as it is to us. And so to give the full name and the location you believe they are in is to make things sharper, clearer, more to the point, in short, easier to work with from the standpoint of that person's Guardian Angels. That way there's no question as to whom the Healing energies are to be directed.

LK   But if you are working with Infinite Intelligence, why would you also work with other entities? It would seem unnecessary.

FM   True. With the Infinite, you don't even need to ask the question. The Infinite already knows the question and the need. But for our own satisfaction and sense of accomplishment, we often need to ask. And because of asking, we do give it more of a reality and an energy to that point.

LK   Are you saying that the same is true for the Guardian Angels as it is for us here on Earth? That they need to be very specific in the directing of energies to give it more of a point and to have a sense of accomplishment?

FM   Yes.

LK   What if you simply visualized the person, saw them in your mind's eye as vividly as possible, and in some locale that they would be associated with such as their home? Would that work in lieu of not knowing for certain where they were located geographically?

FM   That's fine. That's fine. Because we can go from point A to point B in a short period of time. We've already caught the thread, that specific connective link between ourselves and the other person, so it just needs to move into the direction of where they are.

LK   Can these same procedures for Healing at a distance be used in place of the laying on of hands even though the subject is right in front of you, within arm's reach so to speak?

FM   Of course.

· · ·

LK   At this point, I'd like to ask some questions about Healing that I, myself, have had along the way, which I imagine others may also have.

FM   Fine.

LK   Why do some Healings work and others not?

FM   In working with Healing, oftentimes, it is believed that the recipient has to have faith in God to be healed. But I've worked with many people who have been, or have considered themselves, atheist, or not to believe in any kind of greater, unseen Power, and yet have acknowledged Healing.

So in my experience, it is not through faith, or belief in a particular system, that any certain individual is healed. For myself, I work with what I think of as an Infinite Source, an Infinite Power, however, I cannot interpret what it is, or how it is, or how it really works. I never know whether a person is going to be healed at the time I work with them or not. Or at any other time, for that matter.

But if all things are right in the relationship of everything that surrounds the situation—the healer, the recipient of the Healing, and all the energies that are concerned with this particular individual at that time—then results do happen, regardless of a person's beliefs, religious or whatever. Results are accomplished.

One of the things I feel strongly about is ... oh, for instance, a plane crashes and people will send out thoughts for all the people in the plane crash. If there is no connection between the people sending the thought and those people who were in the plane crash, there's nothing much that the Energy can do, because there are no connecting links.

Now I'm not saying it's not a good idea, I am simply saying we need connecting threads with others to make a real connecting point of contact for this Infinite Intelligence to work through. Otherwise, the Intelligence works, but its utilization is from those who are connected with those who went down in the airplane, not with those who have no connection with the circumstances. If it makes the individual feel better to do so, fine, but I would be very surprised to learn that there would be much of a result in such a case.

LK   We've been talking here about a connecting link, or a thread, between individuals. Maybe this should be explained before we go any further.

FM   There is a connection, or points of contact, between individuals, that are often perceived and referred to as "threads." Now these threads could be very weak between two people who have met once, discussed the weather, but had little interest in each other. But as you get to know an individual, more and more, these "threads" grow stronger. An Energy, a Power, an Intelligence is built between those two individuals in such a way that there's a greater validity between them. And where there are such threads between two people, the processes of Healing are enhanced.

LK   I've heard you say that in Healing your procedure is the same whether it's a common cold or cancer. In other words, you do what you do and beyond that point you have no real responsibility. Is that so?

FM   Yes.

LK   This brings up the question of how long might a person

expect to wait to see results from a Healing session. That is, are Healings mostly instantaneous, or do they progress over a period of time?

FM   Instantaneous Healings are possible, but in my experience immediate results seldom happen. Usually results are overnight. I think there's a process that takes place while the individual is sleeping. I can't scientifically prove it, but it seems that by the next day they may not even be aware that they've received help. But through the course of the day they might say, `Oh, it's gone!' or, `I'm feeling much better today. How about that.'

LK   So more often than not, one just has to wait and see?

FM   Right.

• • •

LK   Would you say that faith Healings are different than what you are doing?

FM   Definitely.

LK   Could you say a little more about that? The difference between Color Healing and Faith Healing.

FM   In Faith Healings the emphasis is on the healer. That is to say that the person in need has to believe in that person, that healer, or in some particular principle of belief that Healing can come about by this Faith Process. Otherwise it doesn't take place.
   But with the use of Color in Healing, I have seen many instances, many many instances, where Healing has taken place for a person who is an agnostic, or an atheist, or denies the possibility that such a process could be helpful for them. With Color it really

doesn't make too much difference what the individual believes.

In my experience and observation over the years, I've found that this Intelligence, this Power works, that it is just there, a Universal Power for all of us. And when it is induced into those who are in need, it doesn't seem to matter whether they believe in anything that I believe in, or have any confidence in something that is greater than themselves. It still works.

LK   How long would one expect to go before they would know that they had been healed permanently?

FM   The longer the better, of course. However, a couple of years without any reoccurrence of the problem is generally regarded as being a sufficient time to feel that a Healing has "taken."

LK   You once told me that I might expect a reoccurrence of certain symptoms, but that they would be weaker or of less duration in time. I think it is important to bring this out, because if some small set back occurs to a person who thinks that a Healing is a one time all-or-nothing situation, they might lose the advantage they have.

FM   Yes, I think that is important to acknowledge. Because many people think they can come to a healer just once (and some healers do feel that once is enough), but I have found that oftentimes several session of Healing are needed. However, I seldom ask people to return in relationship to Healing.

LK   You wouldn't tell them? Would that be because telling them might undermine their confidence in the work done?

FM   Yes. It's up to them to come back if it is needed. If they ask, then we go from that particular point.

LK   You're saying, then, that in most instances one session with a person is not enough?

FM   That's right. Because, you know, it's taken a long time for them to create that dis-ease, and it usually takes a little time for something to diminish. That doesn't mean that it can't be done instantaneously, but in my experience I've found it takes a bit of time.

. . .

LK   To return to Self-Healing, can an individual ask for and receive help from the other side? By the other side, I mean those loved ones who have passed from this earthly existence for the next world, or the world beyond this world?

FM   We do have assistance from the other side if we are willing to take advantage of it. We all have Guardian Angels, you might say, on the other side. Those Guardian Angels are usually loved ones. Friends who want to help us, give us understanding and direction. Love attracts and they are still very close to us, they care about us, they care about what we're doing, what's going on in our life. But it's not a daily thing. It's not that they're going to tell us what to do at every turn of our life. They're just the same as friends here on Earth side. However, if we're open and receptive, they will help us by a word or a phrase of advice. This is usually perceived as a feeling or a thought which we will probably think of as our own. Sort of a strong hunch that you are moving in the right direction.

LK   Just now you used the term "Guardian Angels." I've also heard the term "Spiritual Guide" used frequently. Is there a difference?

FM   A Guide is usually with their particular individual all of the time. That's number one. For instance Ford's control, Fletcher, told him that he would be there for the duration of Ford's life time. And usually that's the way it is, though not always.

It's really dependent on the Guide assuming that the one he is with is learning in the Spiritual fields, that he really means business. And so such persons do have a specific Guide.

Most people are seeking but not delving into it. And so loved ones are usually able to help them along the way, whereas with a Guide there is more the sense of a teacher, a one on one circumstance.

. . .

LK   Who can heal and who can't?

FM   Anyone can heal. It's a talent like any other. Practice is what is needed.

LK   Like playing the piano. Anyone might learn to play the piano to some extent, but only a few become virtuosos.

FM   Exactly. But remember, those who are virtuosos, those who enter into this life as prodigies in whatever, are not there by accident, or purely on the basis of heredity, they are where they are because of work done in previous lives.

LK   How is it that some people, in Healing others, are energized and others depleted. In other words, how does one assure that one doesn't use one's own energies, but the energies that are always around us?

FM   I think primarily that those who become depleted after the treatment of one or two people are not really that comfortable with what they are doing. We need to be very relaxed, we need to be very confident in knowing that the Universe is already there, and that it is perfect. That way we don't have the feeling that we personally have to put something back into place for the other individual. We are only a conduit, a channel, for the in-coming and out-going energies. In that manner all things surrounding the Healing session are well balanced. I suppose it is greatly a matter of experience in relaxation.

For example, it is not necessary for me to know what the condition, or circumstances are with the person who has come to me for help, because if we're working with this Infinite resource, which we are, it already knows. This Power, which is readily accessible, knows what needs to be worked upon. So all we do is try to settle in with this understanding and be comfortable with the totality of the situation, and not try to hold to the dis-ease of circumstance or condition. We're just trying to work with this very perfect World, this very perfect Universe, this very perfect Power. And that is when the healer, himself, may experience an energizing effect, as well.

However, if someone needs to release their situation by naming it, or telling what it is that troubles them, fine, they do so, and we go from there.

LK What I've learned from you about Healing is to work with a person by the laying on of hands, or in the case of absent Healing, by surrounding that person, in my mind's eye, with White Light, or a Color; however, this process takes a few minutes if it is to be effective. Yet I have experienced highly effective Healing energies from you, that you seemed to have tossed off in an instant and gone on with whatever else you were doing. How are you able to do that?

FM Practice. Again, I'd like to say, that if you are in the flow, or movement of the Power, it just is. It's not something you get into or you get out of as long as at that moment you are aware of the Infinite, the Universal Perfect Energy.

LK   It seems then, that Healing is largely a matter of wanting to do so and letting it happen.

FM   Absolutely.

PART SEVEN
Exorcism and Protection

LK I know that you once had problems after healing a person who was suicidal. They were healed, but you were affected and experienced suicidal urges for some time after that. If Healing is safe for anyone to practice, how could this problem have come about?

FM I didn't protect myself.

LK But I've heard you say, more than once, that there is nothing to fear. And that any Healing or Good Thought sent out cannot possible harm the recipient or the one directing the Energy.

FM That's correct. But in this case, I am speaking of an Exorcism. In that, one has to know what one is doing. This is not something you do at first.

LK How is the kind of Healing we have just spoken of different from Exorcism?

FM With Exorcism, we are working not only with a troubled person, who is in the flesh, but also with an entity who is out of the flesh. Someone who has passed on and remains in a troubled state of thought, and who for one reason or another has attached themselves to a person in the flesh. It is this separation, this working with two entities, one in this world, one in the unseen world, that compounds the demands on the healer's knowledge and skill. Especially this working with an unseen, unknown entity, whose specific energy, or condition, we usually know nothing about.

That was the case of the man with the suicidal urges. He was being afflicted by someone on the other side, who had come to him and worked him into this position, which I didn't realize at the time. Therefore I was working with something that at that time I had not been sufficiently trained to do. And so, therefore, it affected me.

LK So in an Exorcism you are always dealing with an entity that is out of the flesh.

FM That's right.

LK Would you mind relating that experience, for the interest of the paranormal in it?

FM I wouldn't mind. What happen was this, I had been doing Exorcisms for a short time, albeit without sufficient knowledge, and this gentleman heard about me, and so he came up. I'd never met him before. So I talked with him, and then did my usual thing in the process of how I worked with Exorcism at that time.

    I worked with him for maybe half-an-hour, and that was that. He left, and I never saw him again. But I did hear through the grapevine that he was all set, he was better. But I evidently had acquired his situation. Because for one year afterwards, every so often, maybe as much as once or twice a week, I would get this terrible sense of wanting to commit suicide. There was no reason for it, it just came out of the blue, and I would literally hang onto whatever I could hang onto until this thought diminished to the point where it was gone.

    During the time of those attacks, oh, lasting maybe two or three to five minutes, I would have this compulsive urge of suicide. In my mind I knew it wasn't a good thing to do, and I knew I didn't want to do it. But it was just like having a cut on your body, there's nothing you can do about it, there it is, and I would just hang in there, literally grab onto a chair or something, until the urge subsided. That condition lasted for about a year.

Understandingly I didn't do much more with Exorcism. Not until several years later, after I had practiced and learned a lot more about it.

• • •

Another time I was careless because I already knew the people, felt comfortable with them, and just went ahead and worked with the situation and then came home.

That was fine, but the following morning I was told by my wife that she was disturbed all night by a voice, and one of my children had had the same problem. So this person I had worked with, or rather the person who I had worked on, who was on the other side, had come home with me. I was not attached to the situation myself, but she had come along for the ride, so to speak. I took care of that right then and there. Again I had been careless. That time because I knew the people.

• • •

The thing that I have found with Exorcism is that you have to be at a perfectly pitched point of feeling that all life is good, that all life is perfect. And that you can work with and go through anything there is, because whatever it is, is just simply an illusionary process. And from that simple text, that's when I know I have the ability to work with somebody with a particular need in the area of Exorcism.

I won't do it unless I feel that kind of state of consciousness, which obviously you have to work up to. I've gone to work with situations and not been able to stick to that point, and had to return at a later date.

• • •

LK   How do you protect yourself? As you said a moment ago, you didn't do much with Exorcism until you knew a lot more about it.

FM   Well, first of all I believe we are working with the most powerful situation in the whole world. Power is a wonderful thing if you know how to control it. If you don't it's a very dangerous thing.

The Power of the Spirit is the most powerful thing there is, and we must go through a schooling process, one step at a time, the same as with anything else we wish to master. If we don't, then we're in trouble.

As far I am concerned, the art of protection is absolutely necessary, especially as you become more and more involved with Healing, or for that matter anything on the Spiritual Path. The more involved you become, the more importance must be laid on protecting oneself.

Protection is simply the art of realizing Infinite Perfection. There are unlimited ways you can go about it. Some use crystals, or certain chants, or the Christian Bible as their bases for protection. It depends on whatever your belief system is.

My belief system is "Total Thought." Thought is the most powerful thing. Without thought what can one do? Nothing. So you build and build and create an Energy, with the support of other energies, both seen and unseen. These energies are felt, even though I often don't know where they come from.

One can use White Light, or a Color, as we've already discussed, or anything they want to, as long as that creates within them the situation of absolute perfection, that feeling that all things are perfect and that anything that seems otherwise is illusion.

You might do this once a day, during Meditation, say, or ten times a day, depending upon how you are feeling, what is happening, what you are going to come up against.

When you go to Spiritual gatherings that's the time you should do it more than ever, because people are prepared to be open and receptive to all the good that's coming in. But because of that heightened sensitivity and openness, the consciousness is also just as open to negativity and that can be dangerous.

LK   I would think that Spiritual gatherings, such as the ones you held at Fare-Thee-Well, would attract a greater percentage of negativity then a more general sort of gathering, such as a concert of classical music, since many of the people who come to special Spiritual services are there because of some life crisis and are looking for help, and consequently (and I include myself in this), they may be giving off a great deal of negativity and fear.

FM   Exactly, and if you don't protect yourself, you're in trouble, because there are a lot of loose happenings there.

LK   What do you mean by "loose happenings?"

FM   The negativities and imbalances that other individuals may be giving off. It's as though our minds are sponges, and that we are receiving, along with everything else, some of those open ended things from other individuals, and the danger, as I've just said, is greatest where there are Spiritual gatherings.

LK   If one knows of an event in advance, I can see how one might prepare for it, but in my own experience, I find that it takes a bit of time. What can I do when something I'm not prepared for is suddenly right there immediately in front of me?

FM   I understand your dilemma, and all I can say is that once you are experienced it is a very simple thing. In a flash you can do it, because you have done it through practice many times. But to those who haven't, I would say take some time in silence, do some step breathing, something to create a protective aura about oneself. As far as I'm concerned, this is absolutely necessary.

And if a circumstance presents itself immediately in front of you, walk right into it without a thought of what might happen. You'll do something, or nothing, which is also something. You've said that yourself more than once and what did you find?

LK I did something, and I'm still allowed to spend money and drive a car.

FM There you are.

LK To continue with this idea of protection, how would you go about convincing someone that they need to protect themselves when they have been getting by for years without doing anything special in that department? What I'm trying to say is, don't we all, for the most part, learn to protect ourselves instinctively to most of life's situations?

FM Where you see a successful life, chances are that you are looking at an individual who has learned instinctively to handle himself in most of his life's situations. But how many people who are just getting by, are in fact being beaten down year after year in their job situations, their family circumstances, or other struggles, where a certain amount of protection, a certain amount of preparedness, would help them to master these situations?

LK To get back to the healer's art and need of protection, if I understand you correctly, you are saying that to work with a Healing Process on behalf of another individual, you need to protect yourself, and that the art of protection requires absolute silence. In other words, you go into Meditation and from there to a place where there is nothing. Your mind is clear. And then you work with the situation of the person in front of you. Is that correct?

FM   Yes. And one of the most important things to remember is to do this preparation each time one works with a different individual. That's absolutely essential.

· · ·

LK   Why do some people on the other side attach themselves to people here, and how can one protect one's self against such a person?

FM   The only reason that someone on the other side would attach themselves to someone here, is because they find some attraction here in relationship to something the person here is doing. The person here might be an alcoholic or drug addict and so was the person on the other side when they were on Earth. There is usually some strong force that is attracting the entity that is attaching themselves to a person here. Other then that, there would be no reason for an entity to attach themselves to someone here.

LK   So in other words, if the person who had passed over was an alcoholic, he still has a problem, but there isn't available the kind of relief he found in the alcohol, but that habit, or the thought of it, is so strong that if that entity finds someone on this side who is so broken down from drinking that they can't protect themselves, then this person on the other side can get in on it, is attracted to the situation of that person here.

FM   That's what usually happens.

• • •

LK   As long as we're on the paranormal, do you have any other stories of Healing that are of the miraculous sort?

FM   All Healings are miracles in their own way.

LK   I was thinking about Healings that are inexplicable, Healings that according to our current medical knowledge are impossible to explain.

FM   Healing has been an interesting thing to me. For example, in the case of cancer, I've seen many Healings. One of the things I've found with cancer, that I can't explain, is this. If a person comes and talks to me before they have had any chemo-therapy, I can work with them and usually it becomes a very beneficial situation for them.   Sometimes they are totally cured or very much improved.   But if they come to me during or after starting the chemo-therapy, I have never had good results.

LK   Never?

FM   Never. I remember one example of a person who came over from West Springfield. She had three months to live, and a gentleman friend brought her to see me on their way down to Martha's Vineyard, where she hoped to enjoy the ocean for the last days of her life.
     So I worked with this person for, maybe, fifteen minutes and that was it. I never heard from either of them again, not until three years later. The friend who had brought this woman to me for Healing came to a service one Sunday, and he said, `I'm so-and-so, I came here three years ago with a friend,' and so forth, and I did remember him, and as this woman was supposed to have had no

more than three months to live, I was curious to know what had transpired with her, and I asked him. `Oh she's fine,' he said. `She's working down in Marblehead.' Well I was happy to hear that and I said so.

· · ·

Now, where chemo-therapy enters the picture, I am reminded of a woman whose family had called me from out of state and were concerned enough to pay my air fare to have me come and see her. When I got there, the woman with the cancer wasn't eating much of anything, as I recall, and was quite ill. But she had not yet tried chemo-therapy.

I stayed out there for about ten days working with her, and things were coming along very well. So I left, flew back, and a couple of months later, I received a telephone call from the family. They said that this woman had gone down hill very rapidly. And I said, "I can't understand that, what happened?"

Well, what had happened was this, before I had gone out there, her doctors had found that she had cancer and the medical facility she had gone to had to get equipment from Denver, Colorado and have it sent to them in Wyoming.

In the meantime, as I've said, I had gone out there, worked with her, and saw that she was doing much better. But when the medical facility in Wyoming had received the equipment and was all set, they called her and asked her to come in and take this treatment. She told them she was doing better, but they asked her to come in anyway even though she was feeling better.

They checked the old X-rays, which were absolutely full of cancer, and they took some new X-rays. On the new X-rays there was not a hint of a problem. Amazingly the cancer was gone. They couldn't understand it. They took two or three X-rays more and found nothing. Nonetheless, they convinced her to take the chemo-therapy anyway, just to make sure. And then she started to fail, and that is when I was called again.

The family wanted to know what had happened, and I had to tell them that I didn't know. And I wasn't able to do anymore with that situation though I tried.

Since then, I've found that if I can work with a person, in a Healing situation, before there has been any chemo-therapy, there are quite often excellent results ranging from the person's doing much better to a complete cure. I don't know why this is, but that has been my experience with the Healing of cancer.

• • •

Another time, when I was holding classes at the Science Museum in Springfield, Massachusetts, I was doing Healings by the laying on of hands, and a woman in the audience came forward and said that she had a friend in New Jersey who had been in a coma for several months. So she was there really on behalf of her friend. And so, by the laying on of hands, I worked through her to help her friend, and what happened was that this friend in New Jersey came out of her coma at approximately one half hour after the time of the Healing being done in Massachusetts. I heard this later by way of a letter.

• • •

Another instance of Healing that would answer your question about miraculous Healings concerned a little girl, about 8 to 10 years of age, who from birth had had a problem with her ankle and leg. There was no bone marrow in the area, so her parents had to get her corrective shoes, as well as braces. Of course she couldn't do all the usual things that other children could, such as running around, hop scotch, and whatever.

And so at that young age the parents thought that it would be good to have an operation if that were possible. So they went to the Shriner's Hospital and found, after having had X-rays taken, that yes, an operation could be performed that would help her condition.

In the meantime the parents heard about me and came up here to the house, and I talked with the little girl, and I think it was probably once a week for about six months that I worked on her behalf.

Her parents, however, were still going to have the operation done, and so they went down to the Masonic Children's Hospital. They had all the X-rays there that had been taken six months before at the Shriner's Hospital, which showed what the problem had been. The doctors at the Masonic Children's Hospital, of course, took X-rays of their own. And they had to take more than one X-ray, because they found that everything seemed to be fine.

This, of course, was very unusual, because as far as medical science knows, bone marrow cannot regenerate itself. That was the idea behind the operation, to take some marrow from another bone and transplant it, hoping that it would grow in the troubled area.

Well, they checked everything out and found that the bone marrow had, so to speak, miraculously appeared. The little girl was all set.

Her parents were elated, to be sure, but they asked what kind of corrective shoes she would need, and this and that and the other thing. And they were told by her doctors that she didn't need anything. Everything was fine. All they had to do was go out and get her a pair of shoes that fit her. There was no stipulation as far as walking, running, or jumping around. She could now play with other children.

• • •

LK   Before we leave the subject of Healing, are there any other kinds of practices that you could recommend that could result in the healing of physical health, mental health, or circumstances?

FM   Affirmations. I think affirmations are great. But I think that the most important thing of all is to create one's own affirmations. It's fine, at first, to use affirmations that are suggested or written out in books. This way you get acquainted with the process, but the real affirmations are the ones that we create for ourselves and do on a daily basis. And I would suggest that one create new affirmations for each new day, because our needs change from day to day, so our affirmations should be changed from day to day to suit the changing needs. Also to prevent them from becoming vain repetitions.

LK   In other words, they should be freshened daily, whether they are for a continuing situation or a new situation.

FM   That's the idea I have behind that.

PART EIGHT
Other Spiritual Practices

In the past twenty years there have been times when a metaphysical concept, or religious precept, though known about, has become suddenly clear and of great benefit to me in the ongoing work of application. In this section, I have asked Floyd to give a spoken, or extemporized, essay on what was for me, an important break-through in metaphysical thought, in the belief that what occurs to my mind occurs to many other minds. This essay is about the Triune Concept of the Human-Spiritual condition, which I preface here with a story of my own first awareness of the awesome possibilities involved.

. . .

For years I'd heard the term "Triune Self," often expressed as the High Self, the Middle Self, and the Low Self. And although I'd give it a shot from time to time, I never seemed to be able to make, or be sure of making, that contact with the High Self, that energy that can inform us of all we need in this world in an instant, and through which miracles, I believe, are performed.

I tried from time to time to work with this intuitive mind and energy for help in matters ranging from simple guidance right on through major miracles. But my efforts didn't seem to come to much.

Then one day we took up in one of Mr. McAuslan's classes the study of Max Freedom Long's "The Secret Science Behind Miracles," in which he relates his experiences with the Kahunas of Hawaii, and his work to re-discovery the meanings of ancient words used by those ancient Polynesian Spiritual Adepts.

This ancient tradition greatly concerned itself with the contact of the Middle Self (and Low Self) with the High Self. And in testing the pronunciations of these words: Aumakua (High Self); uhane (middle self); and unihipili (low self), I felt, more than once, a heightening of energy.

I have presumed then and now that my High Self was alerting me to something new that I needed and was ready for. And, indeed, I have found this concept of a Triune Self to be of great value. Not that I believe it is the end of knowledge on how the human mind works, but that it has been for me a blueprint, if you like, a concept to work with.

Another of Max Freedom Long's books, "Self-Suggestion" goes into great detail on how to visualize, breathe, and direct your conscious thought to make that all important connection with the High Self. The essence of this has been covered by Mr. McAuslan in Part Two, under Concentration, page 26.

But I am asking Floyd to speak a bit more about this triune concept of the Human-Spiritual condition, because of the great value I have found in it. This High Self, to my way of thinking, can be thought of as the In-dwelling God, or the Christ consciousness in all of us, but I'll let Floyd take over from here.

• • •

- 2 -
Triune Self

The following is an extemporized essay by Floyd McAuslan.

• • •

To think in terms of the Triune Self is really a very simple but excellent way of understanding our mental and Spiritual makeup. It is to realize that we have a High Self, a Middle self, and a Low self. We don't have to call them the `high,' `middle,' and `low,' of course, because none of them are greater or lesser than the others. This is simply a graphic expression.

Our High Self is our consciousness of the Infinite, the total wisdom of it.

Our Middle Self is made up of those things which we interpret in our conscious mind and express through our speaking ability.

Our Low Self is the power house that runs the body, stores the memories, creates the emotions, and manifests whatever it is given to work with.

Because of this wonderful power of the Low Self, what we think, what we say, and what we share with others, is the most emphatic event of our life here on the planet Earth. Simply because this is how we program our Low Self, which, once programmed, is compelled to move toward manifestation.

We are a vehicle and what we do with that vehicle is up to us. We take care of it, we work with it, and so forth. We should realize that the mind is the motor, and that with that motor we make our whole being work. The very cells of our being are intelligent in their own way and respond to our conscious thought. How we are thinking, what we are doing, that is the motivation for them to work and have their being.

It's as though our thoughts are the gasoline in our individual vehicle. We put good thoughts into our vehicle and we can go for a long time and move smoothly. If we put an inferior gasoline, or low octane thoughts, into our mental gas tank, we will find that we are not moving along so smoothly, that we are not performing as well as we should.

If we're not feeling well when we wake in the morning, and we say and continue to say, "Oh, I don't feel right today," each of our cells are thinking, "You know, I'm in pretty rough shape today." But if we know it is going to be a good day, then the cells will respond in like manner. Being positive, however, is more than being cheerful on the surface, or dreamy about life. It is a straightforward matter of living intelligently.

So the thoughts of our vehicle are the gasoline that goes through us. And through the quality of that gasoline, we find ourselves transported to where we find ourselves today. When we look around us, what do we see? Are things working for us? Are we manifesting things to our liking? How's our health? What are the circumstances that surround us?

Whether good or not so good, we should keep in mind that, regardless of what is happening to us, it is not just at this moment that we are in a particular circumstance. It is through the fullness of our life that we have come to this particular position.

By the fullness of our life, I mean the weaving and interweaving of not only our past and present thoughts of this life, but of the attitudes brought with us when we entered this life. Because I do believe that we come into this life with experiences from previous lives and that, whatever those experiences and beliefs are, the Low Self has them well formed.

I believe, too, that before we entered into this life, we knew what our challenges were to be. We knew what we needed to do. We have, I believe, made the choice to enter into the life of this planet Earth. We have, in fact, even made a choice by way of parentage, choosing a situation we believed to be our best opportunity for growth. And so once into this life we have to make and follow the proper decisions to meet our specific challenges. It is a choice that we have, not because we have to, but because we want to. That's why we decided to come here in the first place.

And so we begin to change. And as we change, we begin to realize that we are changing the ideas we already have with new ideas from our Middle Self.

Even though we have in our Low Self the knowledge of things gained of our past lives, it is important at this point that we be primarily concerned with the things that we have gained of this current life in and of the five sense world, and how we interpret things, and most of all how we share them.

I believe that in the beginning all life is perfect, and the circumstances we find ourselves in (from the smallest to the greatest), are what we have done with our perfected state. The perfection doesn't change, it is our concept, our human mechanism of thought, that changes. We accept or reject usually by association and what we are associated with. If we associate ourselves with limitation, we find limitation all around us. If we associate ourselves with the things of good report, we will be associate with that.

The things that we become aware of, the things that we see around us—are they special? Are they unique? Are they different? If not, are we willing to make the changes in our current Thought Processes so that the Low Self can change the limited thoughts we have put there in the past? For example, we speak of "disease," a word over laden with the connotations of fear, when we could be saying, "dis-ease." It is so important to say a "dis-ease" because that's all it is. A dis-ease can be changed. We have the opportunity to change it.

And this is why we are here on planet Earth. To be exposed to all kinds of conditions and circumstances so that we can grow, for we have also brought with us the qualification and the ability to grow.

At first it's difficult for the Low Self to adjust to, or digest, changes because we have been taught from childhood on certain rules and rigid regulations, when in truth, the Spiritual Path is flexible, open, and creative, though most of us, most of the time, are not aware of this consciously.

This Low Self Source is always most comfortable with what it, or what we, are most familiar with, even to the extent of staying with a painful position in life. For when it, or we, are presented with an unfamiliar idea or situation it becomes hesitant. We become hesitant, our ideas become hesitant. In short, we become fearful of change, fearful of the new.

And that is why, as I have already discussed, it is so essential to tune in to the High Self through a Meditation process on a daily basis. Because our Middle Self needs daily attunement with the Universal Consciousness, which is the purity and the clarity of Truth, in order to handle the processes of our desires, our wishes, and the essential needs of this lifetime's creativity. We need this attunement to function at our best.

Truth is for us. Truth is with us. Truth is us. And each of us interprets Truth in a different way. As each of us has a different vehicle to work with.

End of extemporized essay.

• • •

LK   Your mention of coming into this life with conditions from previous experience suggests a belief in the concept of reincarnation. Do you and why do you believe in reincarnation?

FM   It explains a great many things, that without it would be not only mystifying, but seemingly unjust. Also, I should like to point out that we are never, or rather need never to be victims of our past lives, anymore than we need to be victims of past experiences of this life.

• • •

- 3 -
Following Your Innate Desire

LK   When I talked about releasement, in the Part 4: Essay 4;

"Consider The Lilies," I gave the Christian Bible text Matthew 6: 25-26 as a prescription to live by. Here I would like to pursue this a bit further. We often hear these phrases: "To thine own self be true." "Follow your bliss." Or the text from Matthew 6: 25-26:

Verse 25: *"Therefore I say to you, do not worry about your life, what you will eat or what you will drink; nor about your body, what you will put on. Is not life more than food and the body more than clothing?"* Verse 26: *"Look at the birds of the air, for they neither sow nor reap nor gather into barns; yet your heavenly Father feeds them. Are you not of more value than they?"*

Now all these phrases and the Biblical text, as well, seem to be saying "Follow your most cherished desires; Pursue any worthy goal of your choice, and your needs will be met." Can this true? Can this be, then, a fundamental Truth of the Universe? And how does it work? And why don't we know this right along? Why do we seemly need to walk off the edge of something before we find it out?

FM The Universe is here to be utilized and understood. Just as there is oxygen in the air, we take the energies of the Universe for granited, we can't see it. Everything we've been taught has to be seen, felt, heard, in short, known through our five senses. But we need to realize that the greatest product of life is not with the physical, but with the Spiritual, the Inner Being.

I remember saying to a group one Sunday morning, that if they, as individuals really trusted, they should give all that they had that morning when the offering plate was passed. I told them that they should leave without a nickel, even if that was all the money they had for the rest of the week. But I also told them not to do it unless they were sure. And only the individual can say that within his or her own being.

There were ten people that did it and several of them lost out. Why, because they had fear. Three of them made it. They gave everything and knew they would be taken care of.

There was one person, I'll call him Jack who didn't know what he was going to do. He didn't have a dollar to his name, he didn't have any food, he didn't have anything. But he gave the few coins he did have, and something came in the mail that week unexpectedly. I've forgotten just how it was exactly. And, sure, you could say he would have received it anyway. Maybe. I don't know.

But it's a sense that you have within you. That's the thing. You have to do it because you know it is right. Not because you think, "I'd like to do this, but—" And that feeling of rightness has to come over you. But don't do it until you're ready. And once one knows within one's self, one will know that one is ready.

LK   Would you say that, even after knowing, it would be a common experience to feel doubt?

FM   Oh yes. Sure. But it's kind of like "practice makes perfect." The more you do it and find good results, the more confidence you have in doing it. We all have to learn our own level of knowing when the moment is right. I could never tell anyone else when the time was right for them. I might superficially think it was so because of this, that, and the other thing, but that would be because of outer circumstances surrounding the individual that I might happen to know about, which would not be based on a sure Spiritual Knowledge. Only they as an individual can know when. And this comes about by working more and more with the Spiritual, through Meditation, through silence, and inner calm.

LK   This is somewhat like a story related in one of the Fare-Thee-Well essays, about a time when I was out of work and didn't have enough money to pay the rent, but was able, while out walking one cold November night, to turn matters over to a higher consciousness, not knowing how I would be taken care of, but knowing, or at least, having a strong feeling that everything would be okay.

FM   I remember that. What you did was shoot out the Energy into the Universe. You see, everything we do and think, we get a return on it. Of course, most of the time, we don't get a return as quickly as we would like. That time you did, if I recall.

LK   Yes. It was a dramatic lesson.

• • •

- 4 -
Essay 5
"A Journey Begins With Single Step"
(Country Journal, Huntington, Massachusetts, Thursday, December 22, 1983)

The Fare-Thee-Well essay alluded to near the end of the previous segment, Part Eight: no. 3; is printed here as it originally appeared in the "Pastor's Corner," December, 1983.

• • •

"The journey of a thousand miles begins with a single step," wrote the legendary Chinese mystic, Lao-tzu, 2500 years ago. Few of us would argue this simple observation, yet how many of us are willing to put its truth into practice?

How many times have we heard ourselves or our friends say, "I always wanted to help people, have an antique shop, or play the piano, but I didn't have the time, the money, the education"? Many times. What they didn't have, I think, was the courage of their convictions, or rather the strength to make that first step.

Fear is what most scuttles our potential successes. Leaving for a moment the picture of a Spiritual footpath and going to the shore of the eternal ocean, we find that we fear to leave the shoals for deeper water, because we don't trust the water to support us. If we are fearful we panic on the water and when we panic, we struggle and are drowned, because the water requires that we trust its laws of support. It is the same with the Universe. It will support us in our efforts, but we must trust it. If we panic, we spoil our state of receptivity and we drown.

We are told that "heaven helps those who help themselves," and it does. I believe it was Yeats who wrote of the Soul "... that its own sweet will is Heaven's will." These and other such statements I take to mean that the Universe will support us in whatever, providing we show that we really mean it. That means taking that first step.

It takes a leap of faith to put your foot down on procrastination and step forth in the direction of your aims, be they health, financial, or companionship. But like a child who musters the courage for, literally, his first step in this world there are unseen laws of assistance around like the outstretched hands and encouraging words of a parent. Note, however, the child must make the first step, no one can learn to walk for him. Like the child learning to walk, the more we persist, or practice our steps, the easier they become.

If it takes a bit of doing to make yourself leap across a sprawling mud-puddle in your Sunday best, how much more doing (read: courage) does it take to make a leap from the certain certainties of a conservative niche into the metaphysical mists ever before us?

Faith is knowing; but knowing, among other things, is courage and persistence. Courage is what we most need to make that first step in whatever cause, and persistence is to keep walking, to continue putting one foot before the other on the straight and narrow of our purpose.

All this occurred to me awhile back in a question phrased in a style less elegant than the aphorism of Lao-tzu: "You mean as long as I am willing to put one foot in front of the other, the Universe will support me?" The question was asked of Reverend Floyd McAuslan of The Healing Center at Fare-Thee-Well in Huntington. His answer was an emphatic, "Yes."

That is to say that if we do our part, a step at a time, the Universe will see to our needs, not necessarily our financial aggrandizement, but certainly our needs, and that ultimately, according to the strength of our convictions, we will arrive at the place we have always wanted to be.

Reverend McAuslan's answer was, "Yes," and I have been finding his answer entirely so each step of the way ever since.

* I might add that this last paragraph was written twelve years ago, and I am still finding it to be entirely so.

• • •

- 5 -
Application

LK In preparing this interview, I thought that Belief was the bottom line, and then I thought that before Belief one needs the correct Thought Process, and now I am seeing yet another absolute ingredient that is needed to turn the intellectual, the philosophical, into a manifest actuality. That would be Application. Could you briefly elucidate the progression, or the inter-relatedness of Thought Process, Belief, and Application, with an emphasis on Application and how to stick with it?

FM The Thought Process is the most important factor to the circumstances of our lives, but to follow through with it is the most difficult thing in life, simply because we are surrounded with so much negativity.

We are surrounded with applications of circumstances that don't even relate to our life, so that we seem to be inundated at times with ideas we don't even want to be a part of. While at the same time, we are trying to apply certain circumstances in our life in a specific direction of good thought, and it is a difficult thing at first.

It's like going on a diet. At first it is difficult because in the first few days of following that diet, we don't see any results. In fact we're going to find pain, because we are pushing ourselves away from those things that we have been so used to. Our palate is used to certain things. And so it is with changing our thought. Our consciousness is so used to having things in a specific way that we have to break away, break the string, break the chain, that binds us to those limited thoughts.

In other words, we have to break a habit which we have created in our Low Self through thought. And as we know, the Low Self is compelled to complete a given direction in thought, unless otherwise instructed. And it really doesn't want to make that change until it is thoroughly convinced of the new direction.

But if we are willing to make the effort to change a thought pattern over a period of time, usually six months to a year, then we will find results.

That may sound like a very long time, but if we are able to direct our affirmative positive thoughts and selfhood of that thought for a year we've got it, we'll have results, because we've gone through every element of the fleshly life, if you will. The different holidays, the different circumstances, the different conditions, if we go through all those things and we still hold to that specific dream, that specific idea, that specific reality, that's when we can demonstrate.

Now that's in the beginning. Eventually we will find that the more often we use this facility for change in the various areas of our lives, the easier change becomes, because we now have a consciousness that is ready and prepared for more application.

And not just one application at a time, but perhaps several. For as our demonstrations become more frequent, we become more confident till finally it becomes a way of life, and that is what we really want. It takes time to achieve this way of life. Things don't usually appear right away. But if we stick with the program they do come about.

LK I've heard it said, that if you can absolutely imagine something so that you actually feel it, then it is really there. But you can still miss it by losing that direction in the waiting time. Is that correct?

FM Yes.

LK As a last question for this section. What about Knowing? After having discussed Thought Process, Belief, and Application, what do you mean when you speak about Knowing?

FM Knowing and understanding the sense of our own being, 'To thine own self be true,' if you will, to have the wisdom and be confident enough to know that the sense that I have within me, is the correct sense to the extent that I will make that a specific directive of either the moment or of my life, because I do know that it is true.

Now that does not mean that it is logical, it does not mean it is the norm, or the usual. Quite often it's contrary to that. It does mean that the individual, and only the individual, has that sense, has that knowing, and above all, has that feeling. That true feeling.

That does not come in an instant, of course, it takes time to know thyself, to grow into who I am, who we are. With that, there is no question, even if we may question it, it is a reality. That's the sense, that's the feeling, that's the knowing. This is why the five senses are fine and adequate in many areas, but the most important product of all is to have the feeling about a direction, about conditions and circumstances, notwithstanding other circumstances, those outside ourselves, those that immediately affect our personality, our life. That to me, is when we have learned the application of knowing.

• • •

- 6 -
Moments of Fear

LK I once heard you say that there are moments of fear, great fear, along the Spiritual Path. What did you mean by that?

FM In the Spiritual Path, one must be willing to grow. That's what a Spiritual Path is, a growing toward the Infinite. We oftentimes go a portion of the way and then drop off and don't follow it any longer. However, there are those of us who are willing to go a little further.

If we are willing to go a little further, we eventually reach a sort of cutting off point on the growth path at, let's say, more than fifty percent of the way.

At that particular point, we find that many things are changing in our life, our friends are changing, our atmosphere is changing, the things we liked in the past are no longer the same. Everything seems to be changing. And as these changes come about, we may find that we are experiencing a certain amount of fear, because our circumstances are so different, so unfamiliar.

I've seen many people, who have been on a Spiritual Path, suddenly leave it and go back into the pattern of their earlier life at the first sign of change. If they do not return, I must assume that they quit just before this point of no return.

In other words, when one comes to this point of no return, it can become kind of scary because they can see that once they've crossed that point they can no longer return to where they were. They somehow know that the path they are on is the right path, but there are still moments of doubt and that is when they experience fear.

• • •

Now, we might stop for a period of time, a week, a month, or even a year or two. But if we, in our Spiritual growth, have gone beyond the halfway point, I believe, we will find that there is something that draws us back to the path.

I know myself, I left it for three years because I just wasn't sure. But I did feel that if it was my true place to follow that path I would return to it in time, and sure enough I did.

We may have became involved in the paranormal, or any aspect of the metaphysical of life, in a curious but casual way, but after that point of no return it is our desire to continue on in spite of any fear.

This doesn't mean that everything is going to get better and better as we grow. In fact, we oftentimes have more obstacles to contend with. It's kind of like climbing and coming to the pinnacle of a mountain. We find we are very high up, but we see that there is another mountain top even higher, and we find that we have to go down into a valley of limitations and fear, once more, to obtain this next peak. In fact, it is usually even more difficult than before. We are higher, the air is more rarified.

But if we continue to keep our vision on the mountain top, unto that height, unto those unlimited resources of the Spirit, we will again find peace for a period of time. That is the way life is, we have our breathing times, and then we have to work, we have to go forward again. This climbing upwards with a clear mind, however, is what we want, so that our growth is always at hand.

• • •

And this is where I think the conflict comes for so many people. So many of us have fallen by the wayside, because the going is rough and we want to take it easy and do things in a limited way. You see, there has to be a burning desire of the spirit within us to the extent that we cannot help but gravitate toward the Spiritual Path.

Now the Spiritual does not mean that we are always bowing down to this or that or the other thing. The Spiritual Path gives us Energy, gives us Happiness, gives us Serenity, gives us Peace of Mind, gives us the things that we have always truly wanted to have.

We know we can't take material things with us, so the things we want to take are the very special things that we have learned and that we have grown with. Objects are unimportant; the power to understand is the most important product of all. If we are willing to do this, we are going to find good news.

• • •

Oftentimes we know of someone on the Spiritual Path that's having a difficult time, financially, physically, and so forth, and we wonder why they have to go through such hard times when they are truly working on a Spiritual Path. It's not that this great Power is testing us, for the Infinite knows what we have need of even before we ask. What we need to do is recognize what is happening with the whole being. If we do that, then these hardships become more understandable.

Remember, we have taken all of the circumstances of the past, both of this life and previous lives, and brought them into the present moment. Some of these things will be good, others may cause us difficulty. It is through these difficulties that we have opportunities to grow.

Give thanks if you have a dis-ease. Not that you want to stay with the dis-ease. You want it to be alleviated or completely gone. The point of a Spiritual process is to be given the strength to go through the difficult circumstances of life in a fruitful manner. This is why it is so necessary to attend to the Spiritual ways during our span of life here on Earth.

LK   Thank you.

• • •

- 7 -
Essay 6
"The Straight Life Has Rewards"
(Country Journal, Huntington, Massachusetts, Thursday, January 12, 1984)

I intersperse here, again, an essay published in the newspaper local to Fare-Thee-Well, as being related to the previous segment Part Eight: no. 6; "Moments of Fear."

• • •

To pass the time in church as a child, I was fond of charting the strait and narrow. The two straight lines of my diagrams sped like a runway passed the byways of disrespect, laziness, uncleanliness, bad manners, and more, to the gate of a distant heaven. Yet for all their careful cartography they proved not to map for me an adequate meaning of the strait and narrow.

I think my basic trouble with the strait and narrow in those days and until recently was its pleasurelessness, its theology of denial. Why should anything so magnificent as heaven need to be bought by a means so mean, so punitive, so stinted?

Eventually, the glint of a new perspective caught the eye of my comprehension. Perhaps my Puritan background, though strait and narrow enough, was like the magnetic north, a little to one side of the true issue.

What I had not learned from my early theology, was that the path to heaven is already a part of, a feature of, heaven, and that if I were on the "true" strait and narrow, I would not feel stifled or stinted at all. Instead, I would find the path opening before me unto a wealth of pleasure and creative satisfaction, not closing on the horizon at a distant heaven, for heaven is not a far kingdom but an immediate state of mind.

What, then, is the strait and narrow if it is not a denial, or an avoidance of the wordily appetites, large and small?

It is, I believe, the acceptance of all that is whole and well and happy.

"But doesn't that require the denial of worldly wants," you might ask, "such as wealth and wine and even chocolate-covered candies?"

"Not really."

"But clearly, one does not expect to find a saint surrounded by cigars, long cars, and champagne happy hours," you might say.

"No, not at all. Consider, however, where there is a meal of steak and potato, rounded off by apples steaming in their skins, there is little desire for hot dogs, sodas, and jelly beans."

Still, you might argue, "What is the saint doing in not having the sweets of life but denying them, or at least avoiding them?"

I would say, "Where there is no desire there is no denial."

Two things cannot exist in the same place at once. Where there is plenty, there is not lack. The saint, having achieved a well nourished mind, is not likely to take on again the cravings created by the lack of a lesser diet.

For me, then, the "true" strait and narrow is no longer the pleasureless diet of denial as I once conceived it, but rather a wholesome diet of absolute and relentless positive thought, which replaces the mean and narrow concepts of denial, as well as the lesser nutrients of the body, mind, and spirit, and the temptations or cravings their lack creates.

By attachments, I mean, the fear of losing the way I have lived: the familiar, the past particularly as expressed in worldly possessions or popular opinions. Holding onto the past might conversely be considered a fear of the new and the unknown, a fear to leave the shoals and push off into the ocean of eternity. Either way, it is the same.

As a boy, my father fashioned a ring for me, using for a setting a button culled from my grandmother's button box. To me it was the quintessence of ornamental beauty. It was an elaborate old fashioned button of rococo design and opal colors, and had an eyelet behind so it was not marred by sewing holes. It was a true joy.

But with the joy there was the sadness that one day, I would outgrow this piece of homemade jewelry. I never wanted not to feel the pleasure of that moment. (Attachment begins.) My mother suggested that I would grow out of it in mind long before I grew out of it in finger size. This saddened me even more for it was such a joy and crafted by my dad.

My mother was right, however, and in three weeks I was a gem collector of another sort, dealing this time in marbles. My pride was now Apache, a nifty brown and multi-grained, half-inch pocket shooter.

Where there is a new interest there isn't room for an old interest. To put your foot on the strait and narrow takes a leap of faith. We have, as a kind of hand railing, the words of those who have gone before us if we want them, but again, we, ourselves, must hold them as truth by the hand of our own faith.

With these thoughts in mind, I am looking down the endless strait and narrow not as a path of denial, nor yet a mean and narrow clutching to the familiar, but rather as a path of acceptance of wholesome abundance; and that to begin this path, I realize, I need abandon nothing, but rather take on the courage of a saint so that I will no longer desire useless attachments through fear.

It is an adventure, I believe, we must all ultimately embark on, and now is always the best time to take that first step that begins the longest and the most fruitful journey of all.

PART NINE
Questions Concerning the Paranormal

LK   What is the psychic experience? Is it a level of growth, a talent like any other, or a heightened Spiritual development? And why do some have it and others not?

FM   You see, the bio-chemistry of the individual is so important in relationship to all of these things. Also the chemistry of the brain. I think there must be wave-lengths in the brain and according to the nature of these waves certain people have this ability. It doesn't necessarily mean that they are wonderful, Spiritual individuals.

It seems to me that this chemistry, or wiring, or whatever, can sometimes be altered by a traumatic event. For example, I recall a story in which a young boy who in walking along a fence fell and hit his head hard. And after he recovered, he was psychic for the rest of his life. There are many other stories of people who have had a head injury or a devastating fever after which they had a psychic ability they did not have before.

LK   You said earlier that you heard the voice of your deceased aunt tell you to go to the basement and dust books. But later on when you first went to the Spiritualist Church, you said that you went greatly out of curiosity, not necessarily to have any psychic experiences confirmed. What was your own experience of awakening to a psychic awareness? To clairvoyance? Did that come suddenly?

FM   No. It was gradual. I really wasn't even practicing anything, it was just I would have it—

LK   Like a hunch?

FM   Exactly. But I wasn't working at it, it just came and—

LK   And you kept track of it, noticing what hunches or feelings were accurate, which ones were not. In other words, you would eventually sense something sort of like a hunch, but stronger than a hunch.

FM   Something like that.

LK   Coming from the New Age area of thought, one hears a lot about various paranormal experiences, such as there being a sound of the Universe. Does the Universe have a sound, and if so, what is that sound like?

FM   I've just been reading in this Eckankar book that it is like the sound of a flute. Well, the sound of the Universe may be for some the sound of a flute. I'm not convinced of it. There is a sound, and it could be considered a hum, or an om, but to me it is a rounded sound that just seems to last and eventually fade into infinity.
   I'm very skeptical of things that are written in stone, for the simple reason that here on the planet Earth, each and every one of us is different, just as every snowflake is different. The mechanism and the chemistry of our bodies are different. Therefore the catching of that attunement which would allow one to hear the sound of the Universe is different for each individual. When standing in a circle, no two people can see the same thing. They see what is in the center of the circle from a different

viewpoint. There's no room for individuals to be in the same space at the same time, so it is going to be different. Similar, but not the same.

LK   What part does the devil play in your philosophy?

FM   Many people have ask me about the devil, and evil, and the conditions and circumstances of hell fire and damnation, and I can't speak of them because I have no knowledge of them. I don't know about a devil. I think the evil that is, is created by man and his limitations in the concepts of life. I've never met the devil, but I have met the Power.

If we desire only to seek life, nothing else, and we don't waste our energies in some other direction, then we are going to find our growth, our change, our upliftment, our directive, our creativeness. This is so very important, because in the next life we move and have our being in the manner by which we have created and have been created in this life.

LK   What about people that seem quite evil to us?

FM   There's no question that there are bad things and what we call bad people. Some people have so cut off the Light within themselves that it is hard to think of them as anything but evil. Yet it is not evil we see, but rather a lack of good, a lack of Light.

LK   What about Christ's casting out of demons? Would you take that to be literal or not?

FM   We must first remember that Jesus spoke to the people of his times—

LK   In other words, the demons might be referred to now as an illness within the mind of that individual, or entities that are troubling that person, as we have spoken of before when discussing Exorcism?

FM   Right.

LK   About spirit influences from the other side, we have talked about loved ones as Guardian Angels, and of what a Guide constitutes, but what about the tarot, the ouija board, and the like. Are they safe for the amateur?

FM   Caution in relationship to the tarot, the ouija, the crystal ball, is very important. Most people who are utilizing them are doing so in a very limited way. In other words, if you go to someone who is foretelling the future, that person has to have a strong, practiced psychic ability to be effective, and most "fortune tellers" haven't the necessary talent or maturity to use it even if they do have some ability.

If they use tarot cards or a crystal ball these things are simply objects that they are using for show, or for ritualistic effect, which they themselves may need as much as their client to create the proper mood. But what they are doing, in fact, is using their own psychic ingenuity, power, or knowledge and sharing it with others. Which is great when the talent and the understanding of the talent is great.

I think, as far as the ouija goes, it is probably the most dangerous, because there are those on the other side that still have a strong desire to be here on Earth side. They really don't want to be where they are, and they, for whatever the needs might be, are still attracted to the planet Earth and the ouija is something they are able to maneuver quite easily.

LK   Such as an individual who was alcoholic when they passed on might attach themselves to an alcoholic here, as we have already discussed in regards to Exorcism?

FM   That same sort of thing.

LK   What about the I Ching? I know a number of people who consult the I Ching who seem to me to be very healthy, stable minded, even pragmatic individuals?

FM   The I Ching, for me, seems to be the one that is closest to the true ability as far as the use of objects goes.

I can also give you a special example of a wonderful experience with the ouija. There was a couple out in Chicago, back in the mid eighteen-hundreds that went to a person who used the ouija. The wife had a dis-ease that was incurable. They wanted some help. And through the ouija, or I think most likely through the woman they consulted with, they were given a very specific description of where they should go.

They were told to go to a particular area in the Midwest and buy a piece of property, build a structure, and there develop a Creative Spiritual Community.

Now this seemed rather strange to them, and they didn't see how this could be done, but then, they didn't have any better ideas of what to do or places to go. So they went out to the Midwest and bought a piece of property and built a small structure on it and created a Spiritual Community.

And this Spiritual Community grew and multiplied in such a way that today it is internationally known and recognized as a respected organization. I won't name it because I don't know how the officials of that organization would feel today about those early beginnings. But it's still there and flourishing.

So there are times when things like that can be utilized. But with the ouija it is tricky. For example, two people might be utilizing the board while a third party is watching on. Now if that third person has a concentration of the mind strong enough, he can maneuver at will what happens on the board. This is why the ouija is such a difficult situation to work with or depend upon. You don't know the nature or the motives of the person you are dealing with on the other side. Usually they are disruptive or confused individuals.

LK   I've noticed that though you have strong psychic powers, you don't use this talent for telling the future. Why is that?

FM   First of all, I am not a medium. What I do is usually in connection with a thought in relationship to an individual in the group I am addressing at any particularly time. I suppose that's because of the close proximity of the vibrations. I am not one to catch thoughts about future disasters or improvements of the world.   For me, psychic perception usually comes about in a closely knit situation, and comes as a very gentle thought.
   I've found over the years, that if I do have a thought, I still might not be sure. But if the same thought comes to me three times in a firm, sure manner, then I feel certain that what I share with someone as an idea, or thought, for them is accurate. Even though they might deny it, I would feel that thought conclusively and would support what I had to say about that particular given situation.
   In counseling, which has been a large part of what I have done through the years, I have had somewhat of an advantage, I feel, in that I can, at times, draw out with a thought, just a word or two, something about an individual's condition that they did not think of or did not desire to respond to. And that has been very beneficial for them, and also for me as a counseling technique.
   But as for telling the future, it just isn't that important. What is important is to live in the Now. To know the right thinking at

the right moment and the right identity of who we are.

The paranormal is not something to be afraid of. The paranormal is something to be in tune with, in relationship to, all of life. By that I mean, we need to be aware not only of this life time, but of our past lives, as well, and have an understanding of how this life is transported into the next life.

I think once a person truly understands the spirit, he or she will not ask or desire to be taken away from any of their challenges, but rather ask for the strength to be carried through them, because then we will have learned that particular wisdom and knowledge. It is only then that we can share that understanding with someone else.

I think that probably the greatest healers of all are those who have gone through many many problems and many needs, because they will have a greater understanding and compassion for others who are going through similar circumstances.

So often people think that a healer doesn't have any problems, that he or she never has any dis-eases or whatever. And I don't think that's true. I think we have to grow through all these things by experiencing them. The greater a healer's understanding, the greater his or her compassion.

LK Earlier, you said that it isn't all that important to know the future. That what is important is to live in the here and now, the present moment. Do you feel, then, that there is no value in precognition and mediumship?

FM No, I think the greatest thing of having talent for intuitiveness, which everyone has to some extent, is that events in the future can be changed. This can be pretty difficult, however, especially when things are already visibly proceeding toward certain likely outcomes.

A medium could be thought of as a person standing on a

mountain top looking down at a canoe floating on a river. This person on the cliff can see the waterfall around the bend in the river that the person in the canoe cannot see. It is in this manner that this intuitive process takes place.

Now if the person on the mountain top can warn the person in the canoe, well and good. The person in the canoe could save themselve, haul themselves to shore, if they were receptive to the shouting and waving of the person on the cliff. Or if they are receptive enough they might get other warnings, such as the sound of the waterfall, or a change in the river's currents, or even from an internal source of information, their own Spiritual or psychic source. But in whatever manner, the person in the canoe has to be open and receptive enough to receive a directive and go from there.

This is what the Spiritual is all about, being open and receptive to the calling of the Universe and also to the openness of our individual creativity.

LK It is often said in New Age philosophy that there are no accidents. And yet I've heard you say there are mistakes. How can this be?

FM There are no accidents in life, we all create our own fortunes or misfortunes, whichever, by the manner in which we have worked the ropes of our own individual life. Usually, we look at this life time only and the circumstances of what seems to happen or not happen in this particular life span, when, in fact, the involvement of previous lives has much to do with this life of ours today.

We don't usually see it in that perspective. We think everything is in relationship to today, and consequently we wonder why certain things transpire, which seem to have no logic or reason that we know of.

But if we could take an overview, see a larger picture of our own identity, of our own being, and realize that we have brought into this life many conditions, circumstances, and situations that are already in motion and are affecting our present life, then we might find more answers to our present conditions, more answers to our life's challenges, and understand more fully where we are and what we're about here.

I believe that just before we enter into this life we know what we should be doing and what is going to be happening to our life if we do it properly.

However, as we enter this life it is as if everything previously known has been blotted out momentarily. Which it has. Still, we have all the aspects of our various lifetimes with us, the skills and talents we have already learned or have imperfectly learned, that is to say, those things we have improved upon as well as those things which we haven't improved upon. And it is up to us in this life time to find our answers, to find our real life plan. And many of us do. But by the same token, many of us do not, simply because that potentiality, that creativeness which we all have, has not necessarily been worked with in a proper way.

It is how we are working with that Divine Source that makes the difference, that creates the apparent accident or the apparent good fortune.

We oftentimes think of something transpiring that's not very good for us, so we say that's kind of a karmic debt that we have to pay, when, in fact, the word karma can be good or bad depending upon where we are in our life at that particular time. Karma is not necessarily bad. It is simply a matter of cause and effect.

If a person at that top of a stairs has an untied shoe lace and falls down the stairs and hurts himself, this is really not a karmic debt, it's called carelessness. We need to be meticulous as far as our thoughts go in regards to the awareness of life and its activities, and what life is all about. It is so very, very important to us to know the Truth. And having a look at the overall picture helps us, I think, in finding the answers to our life.

In relationship to Fletcher (and I had a wonderful privilege to be able to talk with him), I wanted to know as much as I could about the next life. But as he put it more than once, we here on Earth side cannot in our consciousness of the five sense world really comprehend what it's all about over there.

We know that life goes on, we know that the activities of this life are pretty much the activities of the next life, however, everything is heightened. For instance, color is far more vivid, far more beautiful, far more special. The tones and hues of life are quite different. They are sharper, clearer, and we just really can't comprehend it.

The important thing is not so much to live in the light of the next world, but to produce a wonderful life in this world, so that the next life will be an enhancement of all we have learned, cherished, and believed in here on Earth.

Because the next life is, as in this life, dependent upon our creativity. And the more we are creative here, the better off we're going to be. Things will be much more clear to us, and we will move and have our being in a creativeness that is in line with our growth.

LK Do I understand you correctly, that you believe in reincarnation?

FM Yes.

LK I'm a bit confused here; you seem to be saying that you believe in reincarnation, but not karma, which I have always thought of as going together, yet you just spoke of cause and effect, which is just another way of saying karma. Could you clarify this?

FM   Karma is a soul act, a situation that is a lasting thing which is absorbed into the being, be it good or otherwise. The tripping and falling down the stairs is an act of carelessness, not an act of soul.

PART TEN
Further Experiences in the World of Parapsychology, Healing, and Metaphysics

Here in Part Ten, the question and answer format has been discontinued. On this occasion, after I had set up the tape recorder and sat down to ask questions, Mr. McAuslan began in the manner following, and I have simply transcribed and edited from the tape we had running that day.

The following, then, is Floyd McAuslan speaking throughout, unless otherwise indicated.

• • •

I'd like to start this morning by talking about a situation that transpired down in Connecticut. This was a seance with Arthur Ford. I was there with ten or twelve others. It was a very hot, humid, muggy evening in August. About half way through the seance a woman became quite faint. She was having a difficult time breathing. So Fletcher, through Arthur Ford, said "Let's take two minutes and concentrate on this person and see what we can do to help." (You see, one of the difficult things about a seance is that you can't take a break. If you do, if the seance is totally broken, the same things just don't transpire again, and we wanted to continue if possible.)

So we did what Fletcher suggested for a couple of minutes, and when Fletcher, again through Arthur Ford, asked how the woman was doing, she said, "Oh, I'm much better," and it was obvious that she was. We all felt a waft of wonderful, cooling air. It was just about a breeze. And it was comfortable from there on for the rest of the seance.

After the seance was over, we went out into the other rooms

where there were other people. I remember saying to someone, "Isn't it wonderful to have the air change," and as I was saying this I was beginning to be aware that the air hadn't changed out there in the other rooms, that it was still the same. And the person I had spoken to kind of looked at me and said, "Well, I haven't noticed any change." I realized then that what had transpired during the seance had been contained within that one room. And that was kind of a special experience.

• • •

Another time my wife, Priscilla, and I were sitting in our living room one evening and the telephone rang, and Priscilla got up to answer it, and she said, "Hello," two or three times, and then hung up, came back to the living room and sat down with me, looking very surprised. And I said, "What's the matter?" And she said, "Well, that was Mr. Leete." Mr. Leete had been a close friend of my parents in the days before my parents had passed on. Anyway, he gave his name and hung up, that was it: Bradford W. Leete. And so we were quite amazed.

The following day, we received a telephone call from Mr. Leete's daughter, saying that he had, in fact, passed on that previous evening. And Priscilla said to her, "Oh yes, I know." Fortunately the daughter didn't catch what she had said. Again, we thought that was kind of interesting.

• • •

Another interesting event, that I was privileged to know of first hand, is the now almost legendary communication from the other side of Houdini to his wife, Beatrice. They hold seances to this day, I think, around the name Houdini and that message. There was one not so long ago on TV, though I don't think there was much to it but show business.

Now with the Houdini message, many of the facts were misread. Of course Houdini was a very famous magician and probably still is the greatest magician that has ever lived.

One of his concerns was whether or not there was life after death, and so he left a hidden message, intending to give this message and its whereabouts to his wife from the other side, his belief being that if there was life beyond, he could get the message and its whereabouts through to his wife.

Now Beatrice did not know the message, nor its whereabouts. She only knew that it existed and of her husband's intent. Houdini felt that if he could communicate the full message along with its hiding place, after his passing, that that would serve as a confirmation that he did, in fact, still live.

As it so happened, Beatrice acquired the support of Arthur Ford, who was in the New York area at the time, and asked if he would be willing to see if he could get the message.

It took several sittings and, I think, several months before he got the full message of what was left behind by Houdini to his wife. But they did find the message and the text of the message that had been given to Ford was accurate to the message found. It was through this event that Ford became well known.

Mrs. Houdini, however, had a very difficult time with reporters and just a lot of people interrupting her life throughout the following year. It was very disturbing to her, so finally, at the end of that year, she disclaimed the reported message, denounced it and went on from there.

Now most people are familiar with the denouncement of the message. That it was not true and so forth. But I have a little pamphlet on the message of Houdini, and the history of it, as well as Arthur Ford's word about it. It was just a very special situation and was what put Ford on the map, so to speak, as being the greatest medium in the world of his day. Of course, he experienced many other instances that were just as unique.

• • •

I would like to share another experience that transpired with me through Arthur Ford. This particular sitting happened in New York City.

At the time I was contemplating whether or not I really wanted to get into this Spiritual work as a avocation or a vocation. I wasn't sure. At any rate, this particular message came from Fletcher, concerning a young man on the other side, who had been a pilot and had crashed about two years previously.

Fletcher gave the young man's full name; he also gave the young man's father's name and the location where his father lived. He wanted to get, very much he wanted to get, a message through to his father that he was still alive, for there was a special code message that he and his father had put together, that if he lived this message would be forthcoming.

And so Fletcher explained to me that this young man wanted me to go to where his father lived and deliver this coded message. I was given the message and then the address, which, as it turned out, was only three or four miles from where I lived. Well, I thought that sort of odd, but that I could certainly check it out. But I didn't know when to go, and when I asked Fletcher when I should go, he said, "Don't be concerned about when or anything else." He said, "You'll know when." And I thought, "Yeah, sure I will."

But some months later, on a rainy evening in autumn, I was sitting in my living room reading when I just put the book down, got on my rain coat, got in the car, and drove over to this particular address. It was kind of a strange feeling. I knew what was going on, but it was as if I were just going through motions of what was necessary to go through.

When I got there, I knocked and this gentleman came to the door. He was a professor of English, I believe, at Mt. Holyoke College. I introduced myself, and told him that I had a message from his son. And he kind of looked at me strangely. And I stood at the door, and I gave his son's name, and I gave him the message.

At that point he broke down in tears, he was so grateful for the message. And he said, "I've been praying two years that there would be some sign, that I would know that my son is still alive." And that was the message that the son wanted delivered to his father—that he was alive and that everything was just fine where he was.

The father was very grateful, and he said, "You know, I would like very much to invite you in, but I really can't, because my wife would not accept any of this," and he went on to say that his wife had just stepped out for a few minutes to go next door to the neighbor's and that she would be back momentarily. I said, "That's fine, that's perfectly all right. I just wanted to relay the message, and I'm glad that you understand the message," and that was it.

To see the emotions of that person, to see how happy and joyous such a thing could make someone, was what decided me to follow the tenets of a Spiritual Path. That's when I made my decision.

• • •

Another incident that stands out in my mind as a kind of interesting story happened right here in this house. My second son, when he was about three years of age, loved ice cream. And he was in the kitchen and I was on the porch, and I said, "Do you want some ice cream?" He came out on the porch and suddenly became quite frightened and went back into the house.

So I went into the house and talked to him. And I asked him what was the matter, and he said, "There's a woman out there," and I said, "There's nobody out there." But he insisted that there was, and he described what this woman was wearing. As far as I could make out, she was an Indian woman, and he really couldn't have known what an Indian woman would wear, he was only three years of old.

So I went out and looked and assured him that there was nobody out there. And so he came out again, and he went running back in the house screaming again, and said, "Yes there is. There's a woman out there behind the cars," and he described her again as being dark of skin and dressed in what sounded to me like traditional Native American clothing. So I said, "Okay, I'll check into this."

I didn't see anyone, but I went out behind the cars, and talked to this "nobody" (there probably was somebody there), and said, "You know, that at this time it is not appropriate for you to be here," and went on to say that maybe at a later date it would be okay for her to make herself known, but that I would appreciate it if she would leave at that time.

Then I went back to the house and asked my son to come out again, and he came out and he looked and everything was fine. Whoever she was, she had evidently vanished.

• • •

We've had other phenomena in this house in which my wife and my children have experienced etherial people. They have seen them or heard them or both—sometimes together at the same time or sometimes individually. I've assumed that the people they have seen were people who lived 100 or 200 years ago, people who had once lived in this house, because this house was built in 1784.

My older son use to hear people talk back and forth, having on-going conversations with one another in the evenings. But as in the story of my second son seeing an Indian woman behind the cars, I, myself, have never heard or seen anything of that sort. I'd love to have that experience of actually seeing, but it has never happened for me.

• • •

    I'll tell you a little story about something that transpired a few years ago. I had a heart condition and I was taking nitros after I'd been in the hospital. This went on for, oh, about a year, but I didn't seem to be making much progress at not having to take the medicine.

    Well, as it happened, I was out shopping one day, and as I was driving along in the car, I had this strong thought of going to a restaurant which was about ten miles from where I was at that moment.

    It was a warm day in the summer and I wanted to get a salad as I usually do, and I had in mind a place that I usually go to, mostly out of habit, when I just felt I should go to this other restaurant that I had been to only once before. It's sort of down an alley and it's not much of a place at all to go. If asked about it, I probably would have said that I'd never go there again.

    But the thought persisted for such a long time, that it was just as if the car drove itself, and I just had to go over to this other restaurant which was some distance away. In fact, being the type of place it was, I wasn't even sure that it would have salads. But I couldn't help myself.

    So I drove over to the place, went into the little restaurant, asked the waitress if they did, in fact, have salads, which they did, and so I sat down and ordered a salad.

    As it happened, there were about six ladies sitting diagonally across from where I had sat down. And as I was waiting for the salad, I heard this one woman talking about her son who had gone to the VA hospital where it was learned that he had a very high cholesterol count, and because they wanted to work on other things with him in the hospital, the first thing they had to do was get the cholesterol count down as quickly as possible, and they didn't know just how to get it down quickly.

But they had a nurse there, who had come over from Poland, and she had said, "Well that's no problem at all. You can get that down pretty rapidly by taking apple cider vinegar, a table spoon of apple cider in a half-a-glass of warm water. If you do that maybe three times a day," she said, "you'll find that the cholesterol count will come down." And I thought, that's very interesting, because my cholesterol was also high and after a year
of diet and exercise, I really hadn't gotten it down that much. It was coming down but not very rapidly.

Also, this woman in the restaurant had said that in about a month's time they were able to operate on her son because the cholesterol had come down dramatically.

So I thought, "Huh, that sounds very interesting," and I went over and ask her if she would repeat what I thought I had heard, and she did. At that point, I thought, "Well, I guess I'll try that."

I bought myself a bottle of apple cider vinegar, and very faithfully every day took it with warm water (just once a day, not three times a day), and sure enough after a period of time I was able to get my cholesterol count down. Within six months I had gotten it down one hundred points, which was quite a feat. Of course, I continued to follow my diet and get in some exercise, as well.

So that's the little story about apple vinegar and water and getting my cholesterol count down.

Oh, the one thing that I forgot to mention was that after a two week period of taking the apple cider vinegar, I stopped using nitros, I didn't need them anymore. And from there on in, I was doing just fine and was off the nitros.

• • •

LK   At this point, Jane, a friend of ours who had been one of the early members of Fare-Thee-Well came by the house, and we had her tell of the Healing she had experienced in regards to alcoholism. The following is Jane speaking.

• • •

I'd been drinking alcoholic drinks for a good ten years. The reason that I drank, I felt, was that I was just so nervous about things. I was having anxiety attacks and was just very nervous. Anything I did, I would need to drink to get through it, church and community functions, or even a visit with friends.

It got so that it took more and more alcohol to get me to go to these things, and even then I would still be fearful in some of the things I went to, in spite of having used alcohol to calm myself.

During that time I had many jobs, and I drank on the job. Hiding it of course. The only two people that I ever told about this problem were my husband of that time, and Floyd. But I never admitted it to anybody else.

I remember telling Floyd about it, and that he never mentioned it to me except once. It was down at Fare-Thee-Well where I periodically stopped in, and all he said was, "How are things going?" I didn't know what he meant, and he said, "You know, with the ... " And I said, "Oh, yeah, yeah fine." But it wasn't fine at all, and I'm sure he knew it wasn't.

I remember thinking, how could I ever stop? I couldn't comprehend stopping, because I didn't know how I could live without it, because of the fears. I just couldn't imagine it. I was getting to the point were I was taking things straight without mixing the drinks, just to handle things.

But at some point, after that talk with Floyd, I noticed that I was drinking less, and that I had gone back to mixing drinks more often than not.

It was in November, I've forgotten the exact date, and I was babysitting two children, and all of a sudden, and I mean all of a sudden, the desire to drink totally left me. I knew it. There was no doubt in my mind.

The next day was a Sunday and I was planning on going to the Sunday service at Fare-Thee-Well, and I couldn't comprehend not having a drink before I went, because I was so used to that habit. So I took a little drink and I didn't even want it. I just moistened my lips and that was about it.

And so I went down to Fare-Thee-Well that Sunday morning, and I never told anybody that this had happened, because it was so special to me. At some point after I had stopped drinking, I remember my mother telling me on the phone, "You've never said anything to me, but I can tell that your not drinking anymore. Your face isn't bloated anymore." And I didn't even answer her. I couldn't, you know, I did not want to speak about it, it was so special.

A short time after I had stopped drinking, I was picking potatoes with the group at my aunt's house, and it was a drinking group, and there'd be a party when the harvesting was done. And I was thinking, "How am I going to go to that and not drink? How could I do that?" This was just a few days after I had stopped. And the thought came to me very strongly that in time I would be able to have a little drink, here and there, and I would be fine. Some beer or wine, that was the thought I had. But at the time of this party, I just didn't know how I was going to handle it. But I went to the party, anyway. I went late, though, to avoid the drinking that would start before the lunch. I remember someone saying, "Jane, aren't you going to have a drink?" "Yeah sure," I said, and they poured me a drink. But I didn't drink it, it sat there all through the meal and nobody noticed that I didn't drink.

I took the drink with me into the living room afterwards, but I didn't drink it. Finally I felt that I ought to put my lips to the glass, and I did—then put it right down again. In the end, I gave it to somebody else when I was leaving the party. And that was that.

As I've already said, I had had this strong thought that in time

I would be able to have a little drink, here and there, and I would be fine. And I have had a little liquor, here and there, without a problem. The desire just isn't there anymore.

• • •

After Jane had told her story, we got to talking about other Healings and unusual events that had taken place in the early years of Fare-Thee-Well. There was one story I'd heard of and wanted to know more about. So for my benefit, Floyd told about the "flying of the kites." Again I have transcribed the story from the tapes I had running that day. The following is Floyd speaking.

• • •

One of the things that we did for the kids was patterned after a Chinese tradition. The idea that the Chinese have behind this tradition is to once a year make kites and put onto the kites, at the very end of the tail, some words or messages about something negative that they wanted to release, the most important thing of the year that they wanted to be rid of.

Then they would take the kites and fly them, finally letting the kites go into the air and disappear, the idea being that the thoughts they wanted to release went along with and disappeared with the kite.

We thought that was a wonderful idea and so at Fare-Thee-Well, one afternoon, we took all the children and helped them make kites. And had them write on the tails of their kites the thing that they most wanted to rid themselves of, something that had been bothering them for the whole year.

That particular afternoon was a very, very calm afternoon, no breeze, no wind, no nothing. Nonetheless we made the kites and tried to get them up into the air, but it just wasn't possible to get the kites airborne.

So we adults said, "Why don't we do what we do best," and that was to just sit in a circle and visualize a wind, just enough wind to get the kites airborne so that the kids could have this experience.

A number of us sat down in a circle and worked about ten minutes visualizing a breeze lifting the kites, and sure enough a little breeze came up, enough to fly the kites.

It wasn't a great wind or anything, but it was enough to get the kites airborne and to finally carry the kites away when they were released.

• • •

(At this point, I broke in with the following question and the interview format is maintained throughout the remainder of Part 10.)

LK How can you be certain that your group thought created the wind, as opposed to the possibility that it came about of its own accord?

FM I remember at the time that we inquired around if there had been any air or breeze in the area. And we found that the only area in which there seemed to have been any breeze was in this good-sized field below the drying shed where the kite flying took place. There wasn't any wind, or breeze, at the drying shed itself.

LK It seems to me that it is often difficult to distinguish between a true Spiritual experience and an imagined Spiritual experience. Do you have any advice on that?

FM No.

LK   Before I round out this session, is there anything else of the paranormal that comes to mind that happened at Fare-Thee-Well?

FM   Yes.   Another situation at Fare-Thee-Well that was interesting to me was this. We had quite a few trees and bushes in front of the building. And we were wondering what to do. Most of these trees had been there for a good many years, but they were obstructing our area of use and also the sunlight that we wanted to get into the drying shed.

So this other person and myself walked the land in the area where the trees were. Our idea was to see if the intelligence of the Infinite Energy could give us an idea of which trees and bushes to cut down and which to leave. We just tried it as an experiment.

We didn't give it much time, we walked the area in maybe twenty minutes. We just took a look without making any definite decisions. That was all we did at that time. Now remember, these trees and bushes had been there for many many years.

Nonetheless, about three months after we had walked this area with a mind as to what should stay and what should be cut down, we began to notice that some of the bushes and trees, not all of them, just some of them, had started to turn brown. Eventually they became more and more brown to the point that we knew which ones to cut down.

PART ELEVEN
The Most Important Thing

LK We have talked of Healing, Meditation, the importance of Thought Process, the concept of the Triune Self, and looked at some of the possibilities of the Paranormal. What would be the one thing you would most what to communicate to others?

FM The first thing I've tried to put across is that there is no such thing as death. Everything is change. If we can get into the race consciousness the term "change" or "passing over," or some affirmative word that doesn't adhere to the connotations of the word "death," we'd all be a lot better off. Because the word death is black.

Some people will say that death is not bad, but to me death is bad because death is black. If you are going to progress Spiritually, you have to eliminate certain words, "death" and "fear" are the two words that loom the largest. Fear being the worst. Whether it is a large fear or a small fear makes no difference, because if we have fear of any kind we put up a wall of some sort, we put obstacles in our path.

However, if we can accept the reality that everything that is, is here with us now, seen or unseen, and that it is perfect, that it is good, that it is simply Light, then we begin to break down the barriers that we have been taught and accepted as a rule, and when we are able to do this, we are then on the threshold of a genuine Spiritual way of life.

What we will find, when bad things do happen to us, is that we will have a capacity to handle them. We will find that we go through difficult times with less pain and frustration then we once did.

We need to go through these hard times with the realization that all things here on earth, as in heaven, are very, very good. We need the understanding that all that comes to us, we have created ourselves, that the hardships of our lives are not because of someone else, but are of our own devising. And as we grow into this understanding, that we create ourselves and all the circumstances of our lives, both the good and the bad, we will also find that we have the capability and compassion to help others who may be going through the same sort of pain and misunderstanding.

LK So the one thing you would most want to get across, is that life is a continuum. Is this because, with the prospect of eternal life, people will be more apt to work on their own Spiritual development, and stop wasting time on blaming others?

FM Yes. Definitely. And what a beautiful world it will be.

LK People are quite interested these days in what is termed "near death experiences." There are a goodly number of books out on the subject. Have you had any experience, yourself, or through others, that would shed some light on what it is like on the other side?

FM When I had communication with Fletcher, one of the things I wanted to know more about was the next life. Basically his message to me was this: `You can't really know something on this side, because it is beyond human comprehension.' For example, colors are much more vivid, light is much more radiant in a way that we just can't comprehend. And he laid emphasis on the fact that we need to work on the life we are now living, we need to grow and understand here.

LK But I recall your saying that Fletcher gave you an opportunity to experience some things of the other side, some of the feelings. What was that like?

FM   As I've said many times, it was incomprehensible. There was no way of relating to it. It had no meaning to this life. The main goal, the main importance of an understanding of the next life is to realize that how we grow and manifest our life here will be the basis for the understanding and quality of our next life.

This life is a tremendous golden opportunity to learn how to grow. We have all the obstacles imaginable here. To ask to be given the strength to go through our problems, rather than to ask that our problems be taken away from us is, perhaps, the most important aspect of this lifetime's experience.

We so often expect things, or someone, or God to give to us the good of our lives, or to take away the pains of our lives, when in fact, we need to know that it is we, ourselves, that give or take away the conditions of our life, for we are the total Power.

LK   What do you mean when you say, `we our the total Power,' and that `we create ourselves?' It's not too hard to accept those things in ourselves and our surroundings that have come out of decisions we have consciously made, but when you say we create ourselves, do you mean all of ourselves, mind, body, circumstances, everything?

FM   We need to realize that we are produced from the original intent of thought, and that the Power, the Energy, are an Infinite Source, and that we are that Power, that we are that Source. Infinite simply meaning that it's beyond our human comprehension. It's the same for each of us as it was for Jesus when he said, `I and the Father are one.' We, too, are one with the Source.

LK   Are you saying that we create our heredity, that we create the very foetus that will become our earthly body?

FM   The physically realities of procreation and birth are processes we have created as necessary procedures for entry into the life experiences of the planet Earth.

However, even though we are produced as human beings, we remain Spiritual Beings. We are still that Spiritual Source. You see, anything that has life has the same attributes and is a perfect specimen of Truth. It was in the beginning, it still is.

But it's as if we have splintered from the original intent because of our individuality. We were, from the outset, a part of the Whole, or the Universe, or the Infinite, or God, and we still are, yet we seem to be individual and limited. The one thing that separates us, if we were to be singled out as a separation, is the individual thought. And it is from this individual thought that we have produced our particular being and life on the planet Earth.

This is the reason we desire within us to return to the ultimate Source, for only there do we find the true balance. And only there are we the True Sound, the True Energy, or the True Color of that Source. And this is why on this planet, Color and Sound are so important for all of us.

We don't always recognize it, however. We become filled with the usual physical attractions or appetites of the five sense world, but that doesn't mean that the Source isn't there, or that it's gone, or it's disappeared. The Source is neither within us, nor outside of us, nor does it come to us, it just is. Always and all the time, it just is.

Just as Healing is there all the time. Healing isn't something that is all of a sudden turned on. It's there all of the time, but we have to do something about it. If we desire the assistance of the spirit field and resources, we must drive our thoughts in those directions.

One of the things that was interesting to me, and this was many years ago, that I had this book on electronics, and radio waves, and the frequencies of radio waves, and it represented the different frequencies by different colors. Since the frequencies couldn't be spoken, they were shown in color. And I believe if we're tuned in properly, we often times can see the frequency of our level of consciousness of thought, and the Intelligent Power that is always with us and that we are a part of all of the time.

If we work with this level of consciousness by knowing that we are the ultimate Power and the resource of all, and that we, in fact, have created ourselves from that thought, we will recognize that we are not something that is superficial, or that is man made, nor will it seem to be that something outside of ourselves governs us, we will recognize that we govern ourselves and manifest what is necessary, just as in the beginning man needed certain parts of the body which we now find to be unnecessary, no longer needed.

The appendix for example, we don't need that any more, because of our life style. But when we, as a race, first entered the plant Earth, we needed a second stomach, or whatever, to survive. And so therefore we created those specifics at that time.

• • •

LK   You spoke recently of changes in your life, but said that your basic beliefs have not changed through the years. Could you comment on that?

FM   My basic beliefs have not changed. I believe in immortality for all. I believe that the world can be a very perfect place, but that it is up to all of us to make it that perfect reality, and that this is true, also, of our individual reality. It's up to the way we view things. Our Thought Processes are the most important thing. Everything we are and have about us stems from thought.

None of those things have changed, but I've noticed of recent years that I have, oh, I suppose the word would be, "mellowed." I was at one time very strong in my desire to attract many people to

Fare-Thee-Well so that they could hear what I was sharing, because the ideas I was sharing had done and still do so much for me as an individual. But I now realize that what my Thought Process has done for me, though it might be in part beneficial for others, it will not necessarily be as beneficial to others as it has been for me. So I am not as strong in pushing my ideas as I once was. I'm not so quick to say that what I have found useful to my Creative Spiritual Growth will be as useful in the improvement of another's Spiritual growth. We each come into the Light in our own way.

LK   Similar, but different?

FM   Yes.

LK   Well, if seems to me, that we have now covered your early years and how you came to the Spiritual Life as a vocation and touched on the philosophy you taught at the Fare-Thee-Well Wholeness Center, which you co-founded in 1974 and were to work with for the next twenty some years.
　　We have, also, taken a close look into your beliefs regarding Thought Process; the techniques of Meditation and Concentration; as well as the processes and techniques of Spiritual Healing that have worked for you. So at this point, I would like to conclude these conversations, extemporized essays, and stories of the paranormal with one last piece originally written for the 'Pastor's Corner' of the "Country Journal," as mentioned in the introduction to Part 4. It is really a story, not an essay, and I've thought it a good ending to this book. You know the one I mean, and if it is all right with you—

FM   Fine. So be it.

PART TWELVE
The Light of a Distance Hill
(Country Journal, Huntington, Massachusetts, Thursday, March 22, 1984)

It was winter and two travelers were crossing a plain to the same distant hill. Night came and they stopped to warm themselves by a fire, and talked with its keeper, a man of many seasons.

The first traveler soon said, "I must be going." The second traveler was more cautious, and he said, "It's a long distance to cover by night in the best of weathers and here, tonight, we have the added hazards of snow and winter winds."

The firekeeper suggested that they wait. He told of a light which always appeared on the distant hill soon after nightfall. He was sure of it. It had appeared every night of his memory since becoming the firekeeper many years since. By this light they could direct themselves more surely.

The first traveler said, "Well, I'm not sure of your light, but I am sure of my step by day or dark." And with that he pushed off into the bleakness of the black winter night. There was neither moonshine, nor star shine.

At length, the light appeared on the distant hill as the firekeeper had said it would. The second traveler, though still cautious, had become anxious for his destination also. He had hung back, uncertain, but now he was certain that with the light as a guide he could brave the hazards of the winter plain by night.

The firekeeper had tried to cheer him, saying, "Your fellow traveler, wherever he is, will now see the light as you do. He will surely be at your point of destination when you arrive." The second traveler was not so sure, however, for he knew his companion of the road to be more likely to follow his nose than keep an eye on the intent of his journey.

The second traveler walked on through snow and over ice, through gullies and barberry bushes, keeping his eye fast to the light of the distant hill. Even the bleak branches of a stand of winter trees could not keep the light from his steadfast gaze.

Towards morning he arrived. The light was a lantern hung high on a post by the barn of a hillside farmer. The second traveler asked after his companion of the night before and was not surprised to learn that he was unknown to the farmer and his bustling wife.

And after he had warmed himself and eaten of the wholesome food provided him, the second traveler went back into the winter cold to find his companion; and when he had found him huddled beneath a barberry bush, the second traveler noted how erratic were the footprints that led to the man's sparse shelter, and how straight were his own footprints of the night before, passing nearby on their way to the hillside farm—straight for having kept his eye steadfast to the light.

And so it is that he who travels the straight path finds first the hearth of man's desiring, and having done so goes back into the winter wilderness to find his errant companion to show him
the way of the straight path home.

And if any would know this parable, let him go out into a field of freshly fallen snow and walk its width, looking to his right and to his left; and when he has crossed it, then cross it back again, this time keeping his eye fixed to an oak or a hickory on the farther side. Then let him see in the footprints of those crossings the truth of these words, that in the years to come, when there is need, he will remember this lore and know to look to the light of that distant hill.

THE BEGINNING OF
"A KIND OF KNOWING"

www.ingramcontent.com/pod-product-compliance
Lightning Source LLC
Chambersburg PA
CBHW071120090426
42736CB00012B/1967